ABOUT THE AUTHOR

IRA HIRSCHMANN, author, businessman and lec-
turer, is recognized as one of America's leading
authorities on the Middle East. He has made
countless trips throughout the region, talking to
people on farms and city streets and conferring
with heads of state. He has made a significant contribution to world understanding by writing
several books, including *Red Star Over Bethlehem, The Embers Still Burn* and *Caution to the
Winds,* and by conducting studies for such organizations as the United Nations, the U.S. Department of State and for the U.S. Chief of Naval
Operations.

QUESTIONS AND ANSWERS
ABOUT
ARABS AND JEWS

Ira Hirschmann

QUESTIONS AND ANSWERS ABOUT ARABS AND JEWS
A Bantam Book | July 1977

Grateful acknowledgment is made to Martin Gilbert and Weidenfeld and Nicholson Limited for permission to reproduce maps from The Arab-Israeli Conflict, History Atlas.

ISBN 0-553-11199-X

Published simultaneously in the United States and Canada

Bantam Books are published by Bantam Books, Inc. Its trademark, consisting of the words "Bantam Books" and the portrayal of a bantam, is registered in the United States Patent Office and in other countries. Marca Registrada. Bantam Books, Inc., 666 Fifth Avenue, New York, New York 10019.

PRINTED IN THE UNITED STATES OF AMERICA

To PEACE
from revelations by
ISRAELI SCIENTISTS
to be shared
with the world

I owe a deep debt of gratitude to
Philip Lerman
for his invaluable collaboration.

I am also indebted to David Konoson
for his untiring research and assistance.

I am obliged to a number of
persons who provided inspiration
and assistance in the development
of this book:

Marc Jaffe
David Rose
Dr. Zvi Tabor
Dr. Abraham Kogan
Jules Silver
Sarah Cousins
Milton Jacoby
Zeev Aviram
Marilyn Abraham

Contents

Foreword

What is at the root of hostility in the Middle East? It is not simply religion, and it is not confined to Arabs and Jews. There is Moslem intolerance of all non-Arab nations in the Middle East which symbolize a threat to the dream of rebuilding a Moslem empire. This is true with respect to the Kurds and the Assyrians of Iraq, the Maronites of Lebanon, the Druze of Syria, the Copts of Egypt, the Berbers of Algeria and the non-Moslems of the Sudan. The most recent proof is seen in the bloody uprising of Arabs against the Maronite Christians in Lebanon, where 50,000 were killed, more than all the Arabs lost in the four wars against Israel. And, of course, Israel which is in the eye of the storm.

At the root of the problem is the fact that the Arabs regard the very existence of Israel in their midst as a symbol of their inability to recover their own historical glory, to overcome their cultural shortcomings, and to become an empire again.

To the Arab, Israel constitutes a living reproach. If a "handful" of Jews could defeat the Arab armies from its vast 125 million population, Arab society is reckoned to be sick indeed. The 1948 Arab defeat was termed a "setback" that was due to corrupt monarchs. But the 1967 defeat against Socialist Arab countries was sheer disaster, compounded by humiliation. For the Arabs to concede that their revolutions in Egypt, Syria and Iraq had not wrought much change in the overall Moslem status was too much for them to accept, especially when the newly organized Arab governments were headed by officers who had experienced the first Arab defeat in 1948.

At the heart of this Arab search for identity and restoration of "Arab honor" is their conflict with the European Christian civilization. The erosion of political status grew gradually out of the defeats of the Moslems in the Balkans in North Africa, in the Caucasus which drove home the superiority of the Europeans. If Islam was considered spiritually superior, it was clearly inferior to European civilization in other areas of strength. In the Arab eye, Zionism is identified with Europe. Israel, with its democratic form of government and influx of Jews from Europe, is seen by the Arabs as a splinter of Europe residing in their domain with a dynamic potential for expansion.

The image of the Jews as seen by the Arabs in their own countries was only as an inferior minority, treated as second class citizens to be "tolerated" or persecuted. To encounter the Jews now as an integrated nation in their midst with living standards above their own from whom they suffered ignominious military defeats is too bitter a pill for them to swallow. In sum, Israel is an intruder, a threat as a foreign enclave in a corner of Arab territory to be disposed of by any means.

The problem involves more than a small state of 3 million Jews fighting against 125 million Arabs for its right to survive and co-exist. It constitutes the severest test, whether a system of democracy can exist as a neighbor in the vast Moslem region.

Is there any visible progress in building a bridge of co-existence between Arab and Jew? Israel's olive branch, scorned by the extremist Arabs backed by the Russians—is nevertheless held out to her neighbors with a firm and unwavering hand. In this hand is a new solution, not derived from military might or diplomatic pressures from outside powers which to date have failed, but from nature in the form of water and sunlight. The advances made by Israeli scientists will enable the unleashing of floods of purified, desalinated water to irrigate the sands in the Arab world, as well as in Israel, and provide that long sought break-through for peace.

I.H.

1

Water—New Way to Peace

What do the Arabs and Israel have in common?

An acute shortage of and need for water.

How has the scarcity of water been a major problem for Israel?

Half of Israel is desert (the Negev) which receives less than 7 inches of rainfall per year. (Arizona, the driest state in the United States, gets slightly more than 7 inches yearly.) Israel's southern seaport, Eilat, has an annual rainfall of only 1.2 inches. Even the capital, Jerusalem, is on the edge of the Judean desert.

How has it also been a major problem for the Arabs?

Most of the Arab lands, which comprise over 5,000,-000 square miles (compared to Israel's less than 8,000),* are arid. In Saudi Arabia, for example, only 0.2 percent of the land is cultivated, and the average yearly rainfall for the country is between 2 and 4 inches.

---

*Israel territory comprises 0.17 percent of all Arab lands.

What constitutes the Arab world today?

The countries of North Africa including Morocco, Algeria, Tunisia, Libya, Egypt, Sudan and Somalia; the Middle East countries of Lebanon, Syria, Iraq, Jordan, Saudi Arabia and the states and territories on the southern and eastern edge of the Arabian peninsula such as Yemen and Kuwait.

How has Israel attempted to deal with her water shortage?

By creation of a national water system, Israel has been able to transfer water from regions in the country with relative abundance to areas of scarcity, so that today Israel is utilizing over 90 percent of her water resources. This has permitted an increase of her area under irrigation from 75,000 acres in 1948 to 440,000 acres now.

What is the main source of Israel's water today?

The National Water Carrier System is the central artery of Israel's water supply. Water is pumped up from Lake Galilee and flows through a 108-inch-diameter pipeline along the Mediterranean coastal plain to the Negev, where it irrigates vast tracts of desert. The various pipeline segments and pumping stations are laid deep underground to prevent sabotage by Arabs. This project was built with money provided mainly through the sale of Israel Bonds in the United States and Canada.

What has been done to help solve the Arab water shortage?

Two major projects have attempted to irrigate the vast expanses of Arab desert. Egypt's Aswan Dam on the Nile River is the largest dam in the world: 250 feet high and 3 miles wide, it creates a lake 300 miles long, flowing into the Sudan. The East Ghor project in Jordan is a 65-mile-long canal running along the Jordan River bringing the river's water to previously arid wasteland. It was completed in 1951 and financed by the United States Point Four aid program.*

Have the Arab nations attempted to exploit Israel's shortage of water for political advantage?

In 1964 at a summit meeting in Cairo, thirteen Arab nations decided to launch a "dry war" instead of a shooting war with Israel by cutting off the headwaters of the Jordan River; mainly the Hasbani from Lebanon and the Banias from Syria which feed into the Jordan River to supply Lake Kinneret, Israel's principal reservoir for her water supply.†

Was this Arab plan ever started?

The Syrians began a major bulldozing operation to cut off the water from the Banias into the Jordan River feeding into Israel. They then came under the range of Israeli artillery, which shelled the bulldozers and made it impossible for them to proceed in the construction of the dam.‡

---

*See Appendix Note 1.
†The details of the decision at a meeting of Arab military chiefs in Cairo to paralyze Israel by bottling up her water supply were furnished me in Amman by Robert Barnes, then U.S. ambassador to Jordan.
‡In 1964, at the border separating Israel and Syria, I saw men in trucks and bulldozers cutting into the Syrian countryside to erect a barrier to the flow of water. I then saw Israeli guns blowing up the canal which the Syrians were building to cut off the water flowing into Israel.

Did Lebanon participate in the water-diversion plan?

At a meeting in Beirut in the summer of 1964, U.S. ambassador to Israel, Walworth Barbour, gave me his opinion that U.S. diplomatic pressure persuaded the Lebanese government not to fulfill its part in the agreement to join the Syrians in their diversion of the Jordan River headwaters.

Were there any regional attempts to solve the water shortage?

In 1953 the U.S. government offered to finance what came to be called the Johnston Plan,* which proposed to irrigate 300,000 acres of Syrian, Lebanese, Jordanian, and Israeli desert land, and to generate electric power for industrial development which could provide employment for Palestinian refugees.

Was the Johnston Plan ever put into effect?

After two years of technical studies and diplomatic exchanges, the Johnston Plan was eventually vetoed by the Arab governments because it contained the seeds of limited cooperation with Israel. Though not rejecting it outright, the Arabs killed the plan through interminable discussions and demands for ". . . help through schemes especially designed for the Arabs and having no connection with the Zionists."† When these demands were not met, the Arabs let the plan die by ignoring its existence.

---

*See Appendix Note 2.
†Letter from Higher Arab Committee for Palestine, August 18, 1955.

Has there been any progress toward solving the water shortage today?

Israel reports encouraging progress in *desalination*—the technology of eliminating the salt from the vast saline waters in the seas that surround the land masses of the world.

What portion of the globe is water, and what portion land?

Three-fourths of the earth's surface is covered by salt-water unfit for human consumption and for agriculture.

Is the desalination process new?

Research in desalination has been in progress for several decades in a number of countries. Techniques now exist for separating the salt from the water, but they have been too costly to render it economically feasible.

What are the two main methods now employed in desalination of water?

Distillation and filtration. At the present time, the only known practical method of purifying seawater is distillation—the process of separating the salt from the water by heating the seawater and then condensing the steam by cooling it. Various distillation methods for water from the sea are constantly evolving in improved techniques to lower the cost and make them economically viable.

What is filtration?

In scientific terms, filtration is described as "reverse osmosis," a method of removing the salt from the water by passing it through a film of plastic material which restricts the penetration of salts. The Weizmann Institute of Science in Rehovoth, Israel, together with others, is working on scientific methods of improvement in this process.

Has the United States been involved in developing desalting techniques?

For more than a decade, the Interior Department office of Saline Water and the Atomic Energy Commission have been exploring the use of nuclear energy to play a role in desalting processes.

Are Israel and the United States cooperating on desalination?

The two governments have entered into an agreement to develop a method of distillation in Israel which uses aluminum tubes rather than expensive copper tubes. This process works on the principle of vapor recompression, which permits the re-use of the steam by raising its pressure and thus its temperature.

A still more advanced method developed at the Technion Institute of Technology in Israel, the Kogan-Rose Process, is known as direct-contact condensation. Here the steam is condensed directly against colder water. This process is unique in that it eliminates the use of huge amounts of metal tubing, but uses very cheap plastic tubes for heat exchange between the in-coming cold seawater and the outgoing hot fresh water. It also operates at much lower temperatures, thus permitting for the first time, the use of low-cost solar energy. Also, the use of direct-contact condensation results in higher effective use of the energy, and the lowest cost of any known process for production of fresh water from seawater.

Are there any joint U.S.–Israeli projects in progress?

On June 27, 1975, a joint agreement was made between the two countries "for the design, construction, testing and operation of a large-scale prototype desalting plant . . . with a production capacity of approximately 10,000,000 gallons per day at Ashdod, Israel." The expressed purposes of this agreement are "to contribute materially to low cost desalination in all countries," to extend cooperation and exchange desalting technology between the two countries, and "to make feasible . . . the large scale production of desalted water for use in arid and semi-arid areas of the two countries."

What contribution is each country making to the project?

The United States will furnish $20,000,000 as well as "technical and administrative expertise." Israel's participation is $35,000,000 and "the use of the land and the existing power plant and related facilities at Ashdod, Israel."

How will the United States benefit from this collaboration with Israel?

The United States will receive and will have available for domestic and worldwide use all of the technical data and operating information from these systems. The plant in Ashdod will serve as an important pilot operation for United States plants which will be required in the not too distant future in the southwestern part of America.

Will the Arab nations, among others, benefit from the U.S.–Israel joint development of desalination?

The terms of the agreement provide that Israel's experience in desalination would be made available to other nations with similar water-supply difficulties.

Is any Arab country now employing technical means to relieve her water shortage?

Acutely aware that the future of her planned industrialization is built on taking water from the sea, Saudi Arabia is having desalination plants built for her. (To quote from a broadcast by Prince Mohamed of Saudi Arabia, "Ironically, in this land of oil and money, there is one desperate shortage—fresh water.") Most of the drinking water for her biggest city, Jedda, is provided by seawater from which the salt is removed in the desalination plants. A desalination plant at the Jubail industrial area will cost over $5 billion.

What is an indication of the desperation of the Saudi Arabians to relieve their water shortage?

They have commissioned a study on the feasibility of towing icebergs from the Antarctic to their country, where the ice would melt into water for drinking and irrigation. The project is being undertaken by a reputable French engineering concern. Tentative plans call for hauling a first 85,000,000-ton iceberg over a distance of 5,000 miles through the Indian Ocean and Red Sea at a cost of $90,000,000. The iceberg would be protected against water, waves, current, and the sun by

18-inch-thick plastic wrappings. The French engineers calculate that the cost of drinkable water from the iceberg would work out to 50 cents for one cubic meter.

Are any cities in Israel now living on desalinated water?

Eilat, the southernmost city in the Negev (population 14,900), with the least rainfall, uses only desalinated water. Three large distillation units in Eilat and four units at Sharm el Sheikh in Southern Sinai supply the local population with its water. The seawater desalination plant in Eilat (designed and manufactured by Israel Desalination Engineering) distills 1,000,000 gallons of fresh water per day. The heat for the necessary steam is acquired from the local electrical power station. Eilat's only other means of obtaining fresh water would be by bringing it down from the north, a distance of 150 miles.

In what way is Israel's activity in desalination unique and exclusive?

Israel Desalination Engineering (IDE) is the only company in Israel and elsewhere in the world to engage solely in water desalination.

What is the greatest use of water in Israel?

Agriculture.

Have there been advances in irrigation for agriculture using salt water in other areas in Israel?

In the settlements of the Aravah valley (on the east coast of the Negev) where only brackish water is generally available, excellent yields of a wide variety of useful crops are now being grown simply by using the proper irrigation techniques with water heretofore considered unsuitable.

What other significant developments in irrigation are in use in Israel?

Drip irrigation techniques are of unparalleled importance in water conservation. The result is a substantial reduction in the need of water in agriculture. Another technique is the enclosure of growing plants by means of polyethylene film. This also serves as a "hothouse," and permits two crops per year, instead of one.

What revolutionary advance in energy research is being developed by Israeli scientists?

At the Hebrew University campus in Jerusalem, a team of researchers under Dr. Zvi Tabor has developed a concept which uses a solar pond. Radiation from the sun is absorbed and "stored" in the pond in the form of heat energy. The solar pond is thus a substitute for fuel.

What is a solar pond?

A solar pond is an artificial black-bottomed lake, 3 to 5 feet deep, in which salt has been dissolved—more at the bottom and less at the top—so that when the water at the bottom heats up by absorption of solar rays, it stays there, rather than rising to the top. In this way solar heat is collected and stored for practical use.

Another solar pond technique heats water in a shallow pond 3 to 6 inches deep. In one design developed by the Livermore Laboratories of the U.S. Atomic Energy Commission, a plastic bag is used as an enclosure.

How far has the formula for solar energy been developed for practical use in Israel?

Solar collectors, made of several square feet of metal and glass, have been popular for providing domestic hot water in Israel for many years. Today about one family in five gets its hot water from the sun. (Israel is by far the largest per-capita user of solar energy in the world.)

What part is the Israeli government taking in the solar pond development?

The government has declared solar ponds a "national project" (i.e., a research and development project of major importance receiving government funding). Dr. Tabor has organized a team of scientists and engineers within the framework of the Scientific Research Foundation in Jerusalem, which he now leads. The team includes scientists from the major institutions of higher learning in Israel: Technion, Weizmann Institute, Ben-Gurion University, and Hebrew University.

The government is also supporting other research and development projects for exploiting solar energy (such as for heating and cooling of buildings) since it sees solar energy as one of Israel's few natural—and inexhaustible—resources.

What are some of the possible applications for solar ponds?

Solar ponds can be used wherever large quantities of heat not above 100 degrees Centigrade (boiling point) are needed, such as in the chemical industry, heating and cooling of buildings, etc. Under Israeli conditions, every square kilometer (approximately a third of a square mile) of solar pond is equivalent to about

50,000 tons of fuel oil annually. An exceptionally interesting application is for desalination, using the new type of low-temperature multi-effect ZERESH desalination plants developed in Israel by Israel Desalination Engineering. A study has shown that a one-square-kilometer solar pond could operate a 3,000,000 gallon-per-day desalination plant.

What tests are in operation for future expanded use of solar ponds?

Dr. Tabor's team now has a one-half-acre experimental pond operating in Sodom (Israel): temperatures in excess of 100 degrees Centigrade were obtained before heat extraction was started to prevent it overheating. On the basis of results of various tests, to be conducted on this pond, a pond 5 to 6 times larger will be built in 1977.

Has any other method of securing energy evolved from the use of sunlight in solar ponds?

Dunaliella, a very special type of algae which thrives in strong sunlight and salt water, has been converted into oil in Israeli experimental laboratories.

What discovery from the Dead Sea water in Israel has led to progress in the conversion of algae to oil?

Forty years ago it was discovered that the Dead Sea is not truly dead. Its hypersaline waters, in which no life was thought possible, harbor specially adapted halophilic (salt-loving) microorganisms—both bacteria and algae which can be converted into oil.

Is the idea of converting organic substances into petroleum new?

For the past forty years, realists in the scientific world have been predicting the energy crisis and working on alternative means of fuel production. In the United States, scientists have succeeded in producing a crude bituminous oil from a variety of substances ranging from household garbage to agricultural waste. However, the supply of these sources is limited, the cost of collection prohibitive, and the end product not very satisfactory.

What was the original source of oil?

Its origins are considered to be in stagnating saltwater lakes where algae lived and died, which according to Israeli researchers might provide the raw material for oil that everybody has been looking for.

Does this successful experiment presage a long-range solution to the oil shortage?

When developed, this system of farming for oil instead of drilling for it could be put into practice over vast stretches of the world's deserts where the enormous potential of the sun's energy cannot be used for food production.*

---

*This plan was proposed by Professor Ben-Zion Ginzburg of the Hebrew University of Jerusalem together with Professor Rudi Bloch of the Ben-Gurion University of the Negev.

What are the possibilities of fulfilling Israel's overall fuel needs through this revolutionary discovery?

Professor Ginzburg estimates that if the experiments come up to expectation, an area of 400 square miles of algae-growing solar ponds (about the size of the Dead Sea) could provide the total fuel requirements of Israel.

What additional advantages are there in the process of farming for oil?

The oil-farming idea is both self-perpetuating and non-polluting. The residual fertilizers remaining after the oil-conversion process could be recycled back into the ponds to help grow more algae.

How can the Arab people obtain and enjoy the fruits of Israel's scientific developments?

Israel formally offered to share her advances in water, irrigation, and agriculture with her neighbors. In a speech before the United Nations General Assembly on September 8, 1974, Israel's representative, Chaim Herzog said, "[Israel] was making its offer as proof of goodwill and without reference to political problems which divide the area." Earlier offers to accept trainees from all countries that wish to avail themselves of Israel's skills in technical, cultural, medical, and other fields were also renewed by his government.

Herzog referred specifically to projects aimed at the use of solar energy in agriculture and industry, linked with the use of water resources in processes of desalting seawater and brackish water in the desert. Such projects represent "the highest degree of water control achieved by any country in the world." Herzog said, in offering the fruits of Israeli research and development to neighboring countries "that the lot of man in the Middle East may be improved."

What can the success of the Israeli scientists in water and oil research mean to the Middle East and the world?

Irrigation of the endless arid desert sands with de-salted water from the vast seas will bring manna to the world's hungry and speed the day when shortage of food will be a thing of the past, changing the very face of the globe—a new way to peace.

2

Palestine—To Whom Does the Land Belong?

What has been and still remains the major bone of contention between Arabs and Jews in the Middle East?

Palestine and its ownership.

What or where is Palestine?

Palestine is the historical name given to a land area somewhere between the Sinai desert and the Arabian peninsula, bounded by Lebanon and Syria to the north, and the Red Sea to the south. At various times, part or all of the territory of present-day Jordan has been included in the roughly delineated area referred to as Palestine. This name, meaning land of the Philistines, was given to the area by the Romans during their conquest of it in the first and second centuries A.D. Although it bore different names under the various empires that controlled it in the succeeding centuries, the name Palestine was generally used by Europeans and Christians. (See map p. 17.)

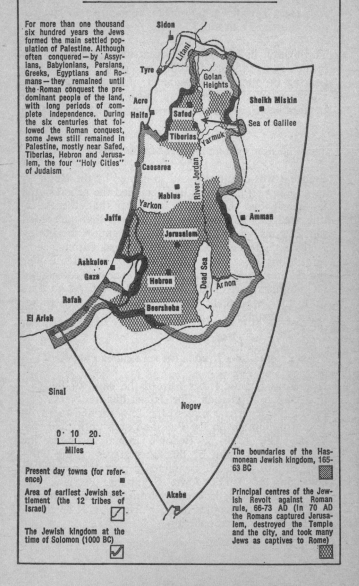

THE JEWS OF PALESTINE BEFORE THE ARAB CONQUEST 1000 BC-636 AD

For more than one thousand six hundred years the Jews formed the main settled population of Palestine. Although often conquered — by Assyrians, Babylonians, Persians, Greeks, Egyptians and Romans — they remained until the Roman conquest the predominant people of the land, with long periods of complete independence. During the six centuries that followed the Roman conquest, some Jews still remained in Palestine, mostly near Safed, Tiberias, Hebron and Jerusalem, the four "Holy Cities" of Judaism

Sidon

Litani

Tyre

Golan Heights

Acre

Sheikh Miskin

Haifa

Safed

Sea of Galilee

Tiberias

Yarmuk

Caesarea

River Jordan

Nablus

Yarkon

Jaffa

Amman

Jerusalem

Ashkelon

Dead Sea

Gaza

Hebron

Arnon

Rafah

Beersheba

El Arish

Sinai

Negev

0 10 20
Miles

Akaba

Present day towns (for reference)

Area of earliest Jewish settlement (the 12 tribes of Israel)

The Jewish kingdom at the time of Solomon (1000 BC)

The boundaries of the Hasmonean Jewish kingdom, 165-63 BC

Principal centres of the Jewish Revolt against Roman rule, 66-73 AD (In 70 AD the Romans captured Jerusalem, destroyed the Temple and the city, and took many Jews as captives to Rome)

Are there specific geographical boundaries to the region known as Palestine?

Throughout its history under that name, Palestine has meant many things to different people. Often appearing on maps as a segment of some larger geographical unit, it has rarely enjoyed clearly defined boundaries.

Was Palestine ever an independent nation?

Before it was conquered and so named by the Romans, several Jewish kingdoms had occupied the general area for nearly two thousand years. After that, the Palestine area was absorbed by the empires that succeeded the Romans, most notably the Arab empire beginning in the seventh century, and the Turkish Ottoman empire lasting from the sixteenth century to 1918. Under the Ottoman empire, the Palestine area was considered the southern part of the province of Syria. At no time in history was there a separate autonomous nation called Palestine.

What peoples have lived in the area called Palestine?

Numerous Semitic tribes formed the basis of the earliest-known population. For sixteen hundred years preceding the Roman conquest, the Jews formed the main settled population in the Palestine area until their dispersal. The Arab or Bedouin influx began in the seventh century, but by the latter stages of the Ottoman empire, Palestine contained a polyglot population consisting of Turks, Jews, Egyptians, Persians, Algerians, Sudanese, Europeans from the Mediterranean countries, and peoples from African and neighboring Middle Eastern countries.

What was Palestine like at the beginning of this century?

A graphic description is offered by the contemporary Arab writer Abdel Razak Kader:

> ... at the turn of this century, Palestine was no longer the land of milk and honey described by the Bible, but a poor Ottoman province, a semi-desert covered by more thorns than flowers. The Mediterranean coast and all the southern half of the country were sand, and the rare marshy plains were dens of malaria which decimated the sparse, seminomadic peasant population clinging to slopes and bare hills.*

Why had conditions in Palestine deteriorated so?

Recurring warfare and the numerous invasions and conquests of the area gradually took their toll over the centuries. Primitive cultivation methods and restrictive customs such as the dividing of land among all children in succeeding generations fragmented and impoverished the soil. Constant local feuding and unending raids by neighboring Bedouin tribes created a climate of anarchy and instability. By the middle of the nineteenth century, a serious decline in the population of the area and in the condition of the land itself had taken place.

Who owned the land in Palestine?

During its regime, the Ottoman government directly owned about 70 percent of the land. Ownership of the remaining land was unrecorded until the passage of the Turkish Land Registry Law in 1858, but by

*The Jerusalem Post, January 8, 1969.

1920 records showed that in the Palestine area west of the Jordan River, 75 percent of the land available for private ownership was concentrated in the hands of 300 to 400 large estate owners, most of them absentee landlords living in Beirut, Damascus, and Cairo. Large parts of these estates were unsettled and untended, with small parcels of land worked by tenant-farmers. Most of the Arab peasants (*fellaheen*) were tenant-farmers; a very small number owned any land of their own.

Why did the Arab peasants own so little land?

Poverty, exploitation, and the medieval feudal system under which he lived combined to dispossess the Arab peasant. He was always hopelessly in debt to merchants and moneylenders who charged exorbitant rates; he had to pay tithes to local sheiks and village elders, extortion to raiding Bedouins, and fluctuating taxes determined by freewheeling tax collectors. Peasants were not permitted to mortgage their land, so to bail themselves out, they were forced to transfer ownership to whoever became their creditor, often remaining to work the land as tenant-farmers. In this way, a few landlords acquired vast estates, and the Arab peasant was pushed into a state of serfdom.

What constituted the Jewish presence in Palestine after the dispersal?

The Jews had maintained continuous centers of population in towns and settlements throughout Palestine mostly west of the Jordan River. From the thirteenth century, principal areas of settlement had been in and around the towns of Gaza, Haifa, Acre, and Safed, where there was an estimated population of 10,000 Jews in 1500; Nablus, Hebron, and Jerusalem, where by 1875 Jews formed a majority of that city's population. Between 1880 and 1914, the Jewish population of Palestine rose from 24,000 to 90,000.

What caused this rapid increase in the Jewish population of Palestine?

In the 1880s European Jews began a migration to Palestine to escape growing anti-Semitism and deteriorating economic conditions. This movement was spurred on by Theodor Herzl's call for the reestablishment of a Jewish state in Palestine and the formation of the World Zionist Organization in 1897 to mobilize political action toward that end.

How did the immigrant Jews in Palestine acquire land for settlement?

Jewish land-buying organizations were formed; the largest were the Jewish National Fund, the Palestine Jewish Colonization Association, and the Palestine Land Development Company. The land purchased was for the purpose of establishing collective settlements and farming cooperatives (*kibbutzim* and *moshavim*). In addition, there were land purchases—mostly for settlement—by numerous societies and individuals, primarily Baron Edmond de Rothschild. Between 1880 and 1947 Jews purchased close to 570,000 acres or 8.6 percent of all the land which was eventually to be contained within the State of Israel.

From whom was this land purchased?

More than half was bought from the estates of absentee landlords, another 24.6 percent was purchased from large landowners living in Palestine, and 13.4 percent was purchased from the Turkish government, churches, foreign firms and individual businessmen.

Less than one-tenth of the total land purchased came from the large population of Arab peasants.

Was the land purchased by the Jews in Palestine suitable for the intended settlement purposes?

Large tracts of land purchased from absentee landlords had been neglected or previously uncultivated. Local landowners sold only the barren or rocky portions of their holdings. The charge later made by Arabs that the Jews had obtained too large a portion of good land was refuted in the British Royal Commission Report of 1937: "Much of the land now carrying orange groves was sand dunes or swamps and uncultivated when it was purchased . . ."

Were these landowners adequately compensated for the sale of land to the Jews?

Hundreds of millions of dollars were paid for the purchase of land from 1880 to 1947. Much of the land was bought at exorbitant prices. In 1944 Jews paid between $1,000 to $1,100 per acre for mostly arid or semiarid land. That same year, according to the U.S. Department of Agriculture rich, black soil in Iowa was selling for $110 per acre.

Did these land sales cause serious displacement for the Arab tenant-farmers?

Those Arab tenant-farmers displaced by the sale of land to Jews were given one year's notice and compensated in cash or other land as required by an ordinance established in 1922.* To encourage land sales, the Jewish National Fund paid compensation or pro-

---

*Protection of Cultivators Ordinance, passed by the British Mandate Government in 1922.

vided alternative accommodations to former tenants at rates in excess of those required by the ordinance.

How did these land sales affect the Arab economy in Palestine?

The money received by Arab landowners enabled them to improve the cultivation of their remaining land, since these landowners excluded their more valuable acres from the sale to Jews. The British Palestine Royal Commission Report of 1937 sums up the effect this way: "The large import of Jewish capital into Palestine has had a general fructifying effect on the economic life of the whole country. . . . The expansion of Arab industry and citriculture has been largely financed by the capital thus obtained. . . . Jewish example has done much to improve Arab cultivation. . . ."

What political event first focused attention on Palestine in the twentieth century?

The Balfour Declaration* issued November 2, 1917, which declared the intentions of the British government to support the establishment of a national home for the Jewish people in Palestine.

How was this intention to be carried out?

As a result of their victories over the Turks in World War I, in 1920 the British government received a mandate for control of Palestine—an area encompassing present-day Israel and Jordan. According to the mandate terms, this was to be the region of a Jewish national homeland.

---

*See Appendix Note 3.

Had the British government made similar pledges to the Arabs regarding independent Arab statehood?

In 1915 the British made secret promises* to the Arabs for recognition and support of independence and eventual statehood, contingent upon Arab help against Turkey in the war. In the discussions between the British and the Arab spokesmen, the area of Palestine west of the Jordan River was not included in any proposed Arab state.

Where in mandated Palestine was the Jewish national homeland to be established?

No specific plan was agreed upon by the Zionist organization and the British. However in 1921 the British established the Emirate of Transjordan in the mandated territory east of the Jordan River, thus reducing the Palestine mandate to only 20 percent of its original size. Transjordan was immediately closed to Jewish settlement, so the site of the Jewish homeland was now confined to the remaining 20 percent of Palestine. (See map p. 25.)

How did the area for a proposed Jewish homeland compare in size to the area Britain was helping to Arab statehood?

The various Arab states receiving statehood on the Arabian peninsula comprised an area of over 1,000,000 square miles. Palestine, the only portion of the former Turkish territory set aside for a Jewish national home, covered less than 11,000 square miles. Calling attention to this comparison, British Foreign

---

*A "secret agreement" was made in an exchange of correspondence between Sir Henry McMahon, British high commissioner in Egypt, and Sherif Hussein of Mecca.

BRITAIN AND THE JEWISH NATIONAL HOME: PLEDGES AND BORDER CHANGES, 1917 - 1923

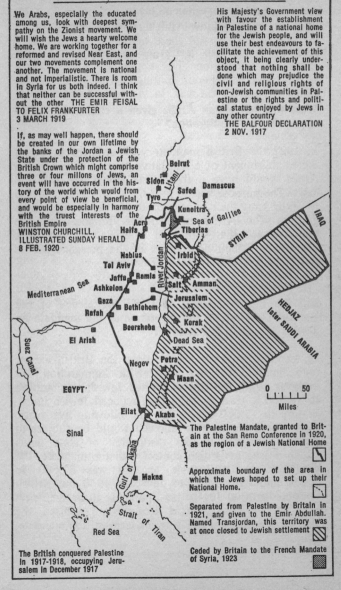

We Arabs, especially the educated among us, look with deepest sympathy on the Zionist movement. We will wish the Jews a hearty welcome home. We are working together for a reformed and revised Near East, and our two movements complement one another. The movement is national and not imperialistic. There is room in Syria for us both indeed. I think that neither can be successful without the other THE EMIR FEISAL TO FELIX FRANKFURTER 3 MARCH 1919

If, as may well happen, there should be created in our own lifetime by the banks of the Jordan a Jewish State under the protection of the British Crown which might comprise three or four millons of Jews, an event will have occurred in the history of the world which would from every point of view be beneficial, and would be especially in harmony with the truest interests of the British Empire WINSTON CHURCHILL, ILLUSTRATED SUNDAY HERALD 8 FEB. 1920

His Majesty's Government view with favour the establishment in Palestine of a national home for the Jewish people, and will use their best endeavours to facilitate the achievement of this object, it being clearly understood that nothing shall be done which may prejudice the civil and religious rights of non-Jewish communities in Palestine or the rights and political status enjoyed by Jews in any other country THE BALFOUR DECLARATION 2 NOV. 1917

The Palestine Mandate, granted to Britain at the San Remo Conference in 1920, as the region of a Jewish National Home

Approximate boundary of the area in which the Jews hoped to set up their National Home.

Separated from Palestine by Britain in 1921, and given to the Emir Abdullah. Named Transjordan, this territory was at once closed to Jewish settlement

Ceded by Britain to the French Mandate of Syria, 1923

The British conquered Palestine in 1917-1918, occupying Jerusalem in December 1917

Secretary Arthur Balfour expressed the hope that the Arabs would not grudge the Jews ". . . that small notch in what are now Arab territories being given to the people who for all these hundreds of years have been separated from it." (July 12, 1920). (See map p. 27.)

Were the Palestinian Arabs given a chance to legally oppose Jewish immigration?

In 1922 the British mandatory government proposed the establishment of a legislative council in which the Arabs would have a five-to-one advantage over the Jews. The purpose was to give the Arabs a legal means for expressing their opposition to further Jewish immigration. The Arabs rejected this proposal because they believed that sitting on a legislature with Jews would imply their acceptance of the presence of the few thousand Jews already in Palestine.

Did the British attempt to fulfill the pledge of the Balfour Declaration and the terms of the mandate on Jewish settlement in Palestine?

In response to Arab protest riots, the British almost immediately set limits on Jewish immigration. As early as 1920, the British limited Jewish immigration to 16,500 a year. In 1939 they reduced Jewish immigration to 15,000 a year for the following five years, after which the number allowed would be subject to Arab approval.* In the disposition of state lands which passed to British control with the mandate, the allotment of cultivatable acreage was 87,500 to Arabs and only 4,250 to Jews. In 1940 the British restricted further Jewish land purchase in over 85 percent of Palestine. David Ben-Gurion accused the British of "not only violating the terms of the mandate,

---

*The British document of February 1939 which imposed the quota, was known as the White Paper.

BRITAIN AND THE ARABS 1917-1971

Largely as a result of Britain's victories over the Turks in 1917 and 1918, more than ten million Arabs were liberated from Turkish rule. The total area of Arab lands in Arabia was 1,184,000 square miles. Palestine, the only portion of former Turkish territory set aside for a Jewish National Home, covered less than 11,000 square miles

So far as the Arabs are concerned, I hope they will remember that it was we who have established an independent Arab sovereignty of the Hedjaz. I hope they will remember it is we who desire in Mesopotamia to prepare the way for the future of a self-governing, autonomous Arab State, and I hope that, remembering all that, they will not grudge that small notch, for it is no more than that geographically, whatever it may be historically, that small notch in what are now Arab territories being given to the people who for all these hundreds of years have been separated from it
A. J. BALFOUR, 12 JULY 1920

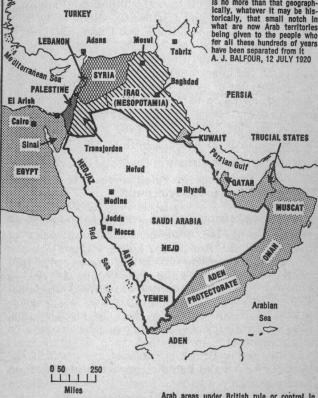

TURKEY

LEBANON Adana Mosul

Tabriz

Mediterranean Sea

SYRIA Baghdad

PALESTINE IRAQ PERSIA

El Arish (MESOPOTAMIA)

Cairo

Sinai KUWAIT TRUCIAL STATES

Transjordan Persian Gulf

HEDJAZ QATAR

EGYPT Nefud

Medina Riyadh MUSCAT

Jedda SAUDI ARABIA

Mecca OMAN

NEJD

ASIR ADEN

YEMEN PROTECTORATE

Arabian
Sea

ADEN

Red Sea

```
0  50        250
|--|--|--|----|
      Miles
```

Arab areas under British rule or control in 1914; all of them were independent by 1971

Former Turkish areas set up as British Mandates in 1921, and subsequently independent (Iraq in 1932, Transjordan in 1946)

Former Turkish areas coming under French control in 1920, but subsequently independent (Syria in 1943, Lebanon in 1944)

Arab states helped by Britain in their war against Turkey, 1915-1918 and receiving British financial subsidies

Palestine in 1922

but completely nullifying its primary purpose."
(February 28, 1940) (See map p. 29.)

What significant population changes took place in Palestine during the British mandate?

From 1920 to 1947, the Jewish population of Palestine rose from 90,000 to 660,000 due in a large part to the land buying and resettlement efforts of agencies such as the Jewish National Fund. During that period, the Arab population rose from 500,000 to 1,250,000. An improved standard of living created by the Jews decreased the infant mortality rate, but the major factor in the rise of Arab population was the great increase of migration to Palestine by Arabs from nearby countries who came to take advantage of the improved farming conditions and the growth in job opportunities largely created by Jews.

How did the Arabs in Palestine react to increased Jewish immigration and settlement?

Beginning in 1920 and lasting until the beginning of World War II, the Arabs conducted a campaign of riots against the British, the killing of Jews and the destruction of settlements. British troops who suppressed the disorders killed many Arabs. In 1935 a group of United Arab Parties was formed which demanded that the British halt all Jewish immigration, prohibit the sale of land to Jews, and establish an independent Arab government of Palestine.

How did the Jews of Palestine protect themselves from Arab attacks?

In 1920 they set up a self-defense organization called Haganah,* which eventually became the regular de-

---

*Hebrew for "Defense."

BRITISH RESTRICTIONS ON JEWISH LAND PURCHASE 1940

These regulations prevented the Jews from extending their land holdings in three main areas of Jewish settlement: around Jerusalem, around Beersheba, and north of Acre.

The effect of these Regulations is that no Jew may acquire in Palestine a plot of land, a building, or a tree, or any right in water, except in towns and a very small part of the country. The Regulations deny to Jews equality before the law and introduce racial discrimination. They confine the Jews within a small pale of settlement similar to that which existed in Czarist Russia before the last war, and such as now exists only under Nazi rule. They not only violate the terms of the Mandate but completely nullify its primary purpose
DAVID BEN GURION
28 FEBRUARY 1940

Nahariya
Acre
Haifa
Sea of Galilee
Beit Shean
Jenin
Tulkarm
Nablus
Tel Aviv
Jaffa
Mediterranean Sea
Ramla
Ramallah
Jericho
Jerusalem
Bethlehem
Gaza
Hebron
Dead Sea
Khan Yunis
Rafah
Beersheba

Land bought by Jews between 1880 and 1940, within the area closed to all future Jewish purchase in 1940

0 5 10 15
Miles

Areas of dense Jewish land settlements before 1940, in which Jews were to be allowed to continue to buy land

Boundary of Britain's Palestine Mandate, 1922-1948

Area closed by Britain to all further Jewish land purchase after 28 February 1940 (4,104,000 acres)

Areas of substantial Jewish settlement before 1940, in which further Jewish purchases were to be strictly curtailed fense force of the new State of Israel. Haganah was used for defense only, and it punished those Jews who retaliated against the Arabs. Jewish restraint was noted in the British Palestine Royal Commission Report of July 1937:

> In times of disturbance the Jews as compared with the Arabs are the law-abiding section of the population, and indeed throughout the whole series of outbreaks, and under very great provocation, they have shown a notable capacity for discipline and self-restraint.

What solutions did the British propose to alleviate the problem?

In 1936 the British government appointed a royal commission to inquire into the working of the mandate. In its report the following year, it recommended the partition of Palestine into two separate states; one Jewish and one Arab.* The Jews accepted the plan but the Arabs rejected it. (See maps p. 31, and p. 33 for the proposed Jewish state, a territorial comparison with England.)

Were there other plans or proposals for solving the Arab-Jewish conflict over Palestine?

The British Woodward Commission proposed several partition plans. The Jewish Agency, representing Jewish interests in Palestine, advanced two partition plans; one in 1938 and one in 1946. In 1942 the World Zionists Organization demanded the replacement of the British mandate by a Jewish state with unrestricted Jewish immigration. An Anglo-American Committee of Inquiry report in 1946 rejected the idea of the partition of Palestine into an Arab and a Jewish state and recommended instead a binational state under

---

*The Peel Commission Partition Plan, July 1937.

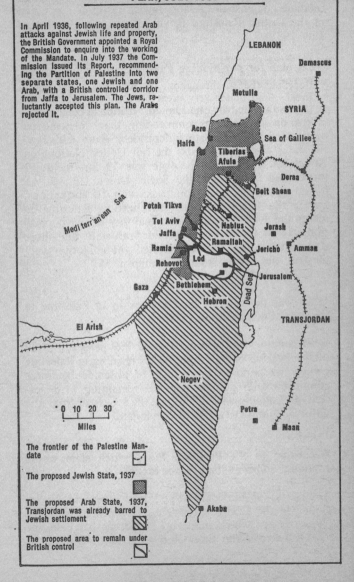

THE PEEL COMMISSION PARTITION PLAN, JULY 1937

In April 1936, following repeated Arab attacks against Jewish life and property, the British Government appointed a Royal Commission to enquire into the working of the Mandate. In July 1937 the Commission issued its Report, recommending the Partition of Palestine into two separate states, one Jewish and one Arab, with a British controlled corridor from Jaffa to Jerusalem. The Jews, reluctantly accepted this plan. The Arabs rejected it.

LEBANON

Damascus

Metulla

SYRIA

Acre

Haifa   Sea of Galilee

Tiberias
Afula

Deraa

Beit Shean

Mediterranean Sea

Petah Tikva

Tel Aviv   Nablus   Jerash

Jaffa
Ramallah

Ramla   Jericho   Amman

Rehovot   Lod

Gaza   Bethlehem   Jerusalem

Hebron

Dead Sea

El Arish   TRANSJORDAN

Negev

Petra

· 0 10 20 30

Miles   Maan

The frontier of the Palestine Mandate

The proposed Jewish State, 1937

The proposed Arab State, 1937, Transjordan was already barred to Jewish settlement

The proposed area to remain under British control

Akaba

continuing British control, with the immediate admission of 100,000 Jews and an end to land-purchase restrictions imposed in 1940. None of these proposals was ever fully implemented. (See map p. 34.)

What plan for partitioning Palestine received the most universal support?

A plan submitted by the United Nations Special Committee on Palestine recommending that Palestine be partitioned into separate independent Arab and Jewish states was approved by the full United Nations on November 29, 1947. The vote was 33 for, including the United States, and the Soviet Union; 13 against, including all the Arab countries; with 10 abstentions. Under the Partition Plan, that part of Palestine in which the Arabs constituted a majority of the population was alloted to the proposed Arab state, and those parts where the Jews constituted the majority were given to the Jewish state. (See map p. 35.)

What was the relative land ownership in Palestine at the time of this Partition Plan?

Jews residing in Palestine owned 8.6 percent of the total land area of Palestine; Arabs residing in Palestine owned 3.3 percent; the estates of absentee landlords comprised 16.5 percent and the remaining 71.6 percent was state-owned land that had passed from the Ottoman empire to the British mandate.

According to the Partition Plan, which state would contain the former state-owned lands?

Almost all of the state-owned lands were to be included in the Jewish state. These lay primarily in the Negev desert, which made up 50 percent of Palestine as it existed at the time of the partition. During the

THE PROPOSED JEWISH STATE:
A TERRITORIAL COMPARISON

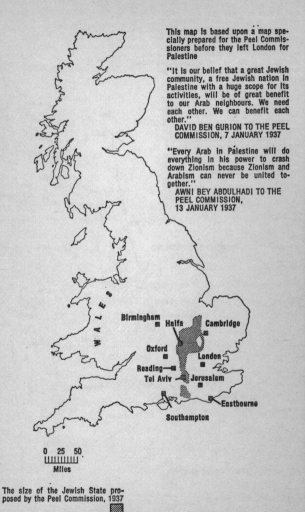

This map is based upon a map specially prepared for the Peel Commissioners before they left London for Palestine

"It is our belief that a great Jewish community, a free Jewish nation in Palestine with a huge scope for its activities, will be of great benefit to our Arab neighbours. We need each other. We can benefit each other."
DAVID BEN GURION TO THE PEEL COMMISSION, 7 JANUARY 1937

"Every Arab in Palestine will do everything in his power to crash down Zionism because Zionism and Arabism can never be united together."
AWNI BEY ABDULHADI TO THE PEEL COMMISSION, 13 JANUARY 1937

Birmingham
Haifa
Cambridge
Oxford
London
Reading
Tel Aviv
Jerusalem
Eastbourne
Southampton

W A L E S

0   25   50
Miles

The size of the Jewish State proposed by the Peel Commission, 1937

Great Britain on the same scale

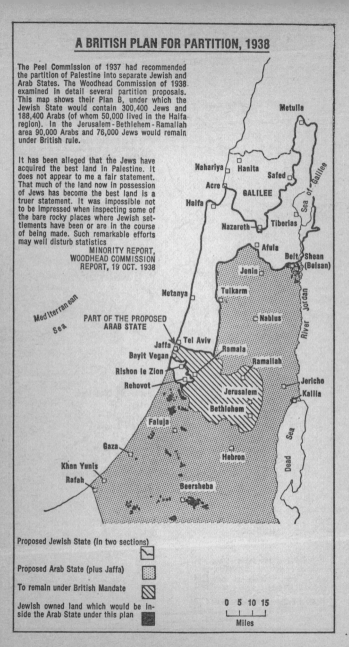

A BRITISH PLAN FOR PARTITION, 1938

The Peel Commission of 1937 had recommended the partition of Palestine into separate Jewish and Arab States. The Woodhead Commission of 1938 examined in detail several partition proposals. This map shows their Plan B, under which the Jewish State would contain 300,400 Jews and 188,400 Arabs (of whom 50,000 lived in the Haifa region). In the Jerusalem - Bethlehem - Ramallah area 90,000 Arabs and 76,000 Jews would remain under British rule.

It has been alleged that the Jews have acquired the best land in Palestine. It does not appear to me a fair statement. That much of the land now in possession of Jews has become the best land is a truer statement. It was impossible not to be impressed when inspecting some of the bare rocky places where Jewish settlements have been or are in the course of being made. Such remarkable efforts may well disturb statistics

MINORITY REPORT,
WOODHEAD COMMISSION
REPORT, 19 OCT. 1938

Metulla

Nahariya   Hanita

Acre   Safed

Haifa   GALILEE

Nazareth   Tiberias

Sea of Galilee

Afula

Beit Shean
(Beisan)

Jenin

Netanya   Tulkarm

Mediterranean Sea

PART OF THE PROPOSED
ARAB STATE

Nablus

River Jordan

Jaffa   Tel Aviv

Bayit Vegan   Ramala

Rishon le Zion   Ramallah

Rehovot   Jericho

Jerusalem   Kallia

Bethlehem

Faluja   Dead Sea

Gaza   Hebron

Khan Yunis

Rafah

Beersheba

Proposed Jewish State (in two sections)

Proposed Arab State (plus Jaffa)

To remain under British Mandate

Jewish owned land which would be inside the Arab State under this plan

0 5 10 15
Miles

THE UNITED NATIONS PARTITION PLAN, 1947

On 29 November 1947 the General Assembly of the United Nations voted to set up both a Jewish and an Arab State, and fixed their borders. The Jewish State was to be three segments, and was to exclude Jaffa (to become an Arab enclave) and Jerusalem (to be an International Zone). The Jews accepted Statehood. The Arabs not only rejected it, but at once attacked Jewish settlements in every part of Palestine.

The U.N. Partition Plan envisaged an Economic Union between the Arab and Jewish States. But in rejecting the U.N. Resolution granting them statehood, the Arabs also rejected the UN's call for an Arab-Jewish Economic Union.

LEBANON

Hanita

Matzuva

Eilon

SYRIA

Nahariya

Safed

Acre

Gaaton

Yehiam

Haifa

Kfar Hahoresh

Sea of Galilee

Hadera

Jenin

River Jordan

TRANS JORDAN

Nablus

Tel Aviv

Jaffa

Atarot

Neve Yaakov

Ben Shemen

Hartuv

Bet Haarava

Kfar Menachem

Kallia

Nitzanim

Revadim

Kedma

Ein Tzurim

Yad Mordechai

Gush Etzion

Kfar Darom

Gat Galon

Hebron

Massuot Yitzhak

Nirim

Beersheba

Dead Sea

El Arish

Mediterranean Sea

EGYPT

Sinai

0 5 10 15 20 25
Miles

Negev

Boundary of the British Palestine Mandate, 1922-1947

The proposed Jewish State

The proposed Arab State

Jewish settlements to be included in the Arab State

Jerusalem and its suburbs: to be an international zone

Eilat

Akaba

Ottoman empire and British mandate, the Negev was an arid wasteland, none of which was ever owned by Arab farmers. The result of this proposed division was that half of the Jewish state would be made up of desert.

Where was the proposed Arab state to be located?

Mostly in the northern and central parts of Palestine, where the more fertile areas lay. The largest segment of the proposed Arab state encompassed what is now referred to as the West Bank area.

How was this plan for sharing Palestine received by the Arab and Jewish populations?

The Jews, as officially represented by the Jewish Agency, accepted the Partition Plan. Arab spokesmen issued a call for a war of extermination against the Jews, and on November 30, 1947, the day following the United Nations vote on partition, Arabs in Palestine began attacks on Jews and Jewish settlements that were to take hundreds of Jewish lives and cost the Arabs many of their own. Military units from Arab states as far away as Iraq unofficially joined in the attacks on Jewish settlements.

What was done to maintain law and order during this period?

This responsibility still belonged to the British, who were preparing to evacuate their mandate, but they did not always rise to it. The task of defending life and property was once again assumed by the Haganah, the Jewish defense force. As the British withdrew from the towns, the Arabs and Jews fought to control them. The United Nations Partition Plan was thus vetoed by the Arabs as they put into effect their stated purpose to drive the Jews into the sea. The war for the possession of Palestine had begun.

How did the Jews of Palestine carry out the terms of the United Nations Partition Plan?

On May 14, 1948, as the British officially terminated their twenty-eight-year mandate, the Jewish National Council proclaimed the establishment of the State of Israel and the formation of a provisional government. On the following day, the combined armies of Egypt, Syria, Jordan, Lebanon, Iraq, and Saudi Arabia invaded Israel to destroy it. The Israelis fought back, and when a truce was reached in January 1949, the State of Israel contained small portions of territory that had been designated for the proposed Arab state. (See map p. 38.)

What became of the remaining territory of the proposed Arab State?

Egypt took control of the Gaza Strip adjoining the Sinai desert, and Jordan annexed the West Bank to its Kingdom to the East of the Jordan River. (After the Six-Day War of 1967, Israel occupied these territories.)

How much land did the Palestinian Arabs abandon when they left during the 1948 War?

Of the 7,990 square miles within the pre–1967 borders of Israel, the Arabs left behind a total of 2,236 square miles, of which 530 square miles was arable land, and the remaining was partially tilled or totally barren. This land was cared for by the Israel Custodian of Enemy Property in anticipation of future disposition arising out of a peace agreement. When none materialized, the Israel Land Authority, which was

THE ISRAELI WAR OF INDEPENDENCE, 1948-1949

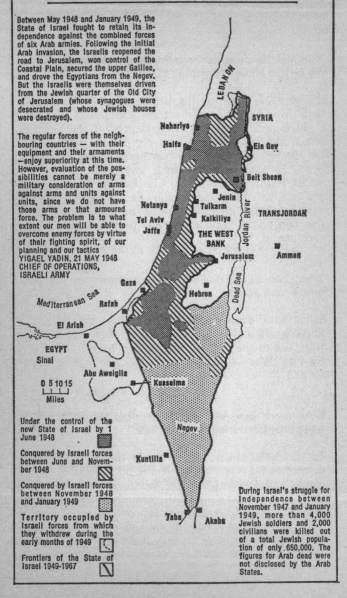

Between May 1948 and January 1949, the State of Israel fought to retain its independence against the combined forces of six Arab armies. Following the initial Arab invasion, the Israelis reopened the road to Jerusalem, won control of the Coastal Plain, secured the upper Galilee, and drove the Egyptians from the Negev. But the Israelis were themselves driven from the Jewish quarter of the Old City of Jerusalem (whose synagogues were desecrated and whose Jewish houses were destroyed).

The regular forces of the neighbouring countries — with their equipment and their armaments —enjoy superiority at this time. However, evaluation of the possibilities cannot be merely a military consideration of arms against arms and units against units, since we do not have those arms or that armoured force. The problem is to what extent our men will be able to overcome enemy forces by virtue of their fighting spirit, of our planning and our tactics
YIGAEL YADIN, 21 MAY 1948
CHIEF OF OPERATIONS,
ISRAELI ARMY

LEBANON

SYRIA

Nahariya

Haifa

Ein Gev

Beit Shean

Jenin

Netanya

Tulkarm

Kalkiliya

TRANSJORDAN

Tel Aviv

Jaffa

THE WEST BANK

Jerusalem

Amman

Jordan River

Dead Sea

Gaza

Hebron

Mediterranean Sea

Rafah

El Arish

EGYPT

Sinai

Abu Aweigila

0 5 10 15
Miles

Kusseima

Under the control of the new State of Israel by 1 June 1948

Conquered by Israeli forces between June and November 1948

Conquered by Israeli forces between November 1948 and January 1949

Territory occupied by Israeli forces from which they withdrew during the early months of 1949

Frontiers of the State of Israel 1949-1967

Negev

Kuntilla

Taba

Akaba

During Israel's struggle for independence between November 1947 and January 1949, more than 4,000 Jewish soldiers and 2,000 civilians were killed out of a total Jewish population of only 650,000. The figures for Arab dead were not disclosed by the Arab States.

established in 1960 to cultivate and develop all public lands, assumed responsibility for the disposition of these abandoned lands.

Have the Palestinian Arabs expressed any willingness to establish an Arab state in Palestine since their veto of partition in 1947?

At various times, Palestinian Arabs living in occupied West Bank and the Gaza Strip have indicated a desire for an Arab state encompassing these areas. But the majority of ex-Palestinians living in other Arab countries consistently refused to consider any Arab state that does not include all of the former Palestine territory to the total exclusion of any Jewish state.

Is there any Arab state within Palestine in existence today?

When the British separated Transjordan from the rest of the Palestine Mandate, in effect they created an Arab state within Palestine. In 1948, when the Jordanian government annexed the West Bank area to its territory, this action—whatever else its justification —reaffirmed the fact that historical Palestine does indeed bridge the Jordan River.

How do those Palestinians who still hope for a total Arab Palestine state regard Jordan?

Their feelings were most clearly stated in the resolutions of the Eighth Palestinian National Council, meeting in Cairo, in March 1971:

> There is a national association between Jordan and Palestine and a territorial unity shaped by history, culture and language since ancient times. . . . The Palestinian revolution, which raised the slogan of Palestine and posed the issue of Palestinian revolution,

did not intend to separate the eastern bank from the western. . . .

The spokesmen for the Palestinian Arabs make it clear that to them Palestine still includes the overall area, which at this time contains one Jewish state—Israel, and one Arab state—Jordan.

Is land still being sold by Arabs to Israelis?

The Israelis have never stopped buying land that is offered for sale by individual Arabs in Israel. Purchases are made by the Jewish National Fund. The State of Israel does not expropriate any land from the Arabs. The 12 percent Arab population who remained in Israel after the 1948 War of Independence live on their own land. This constitutes 20 percent of the land in Israel (not including the occupied territory) which still remains in the hands of the Arabs in Israel. It is some of this land in the Negev and principally in the Galil (north) area that is being bought from the Arabs by the Jewish National Fund at increasingly higher prices.

How has the acquisition and conversion of this land affected the economy of Israel?

Developing the vast areas of barren land put a severe brake on the Israel economy. The Jewish National Fund introduced intensive cultivation of the soil to produce crops of fruits and vegetables—now often four times annually—much of it for export to European and American markets.

What was one of the Jewish National Fund's most significant achievements in Israel?

The cleansing and transformation of the Huleh Valley adjacent to Syria from an infested swamp (including buffalo) to the most fertile area for agriculture constitutes one of Israel's most valuable assets. It also serves as an essential military rampart against Syria.

Are Israeli settlements in the so-called occupied territories illegal?

All of the areas in question—the West Bank, the Gaza Strip, and the Golan Heights—had been part of Palestine as this region was demarcated at the time of the Palestine mandate which opened settlement to the Jews. As they had done with Jordan in 1921, the British arbitrarily separated the Golan Heights from the Palestine Mandate and ceded it to the French mandate* of Syria in 1923. Considered from that point of view, all of these settlements exist within the boundaries of a Palestine officially recognized in the twentieth century. However, questions have been raised about these settlements as an obstacle to a final peace settlement.

What has been the legacy of Arab refusal to share Palestine with Jews?

Four bloody wars, extremely costly in life and property to both sides, and the creation of a dilemma that continues to defy reasonable solution.

*The territory that is now Syria and Lebanon which was mandated to the French at the time of the British mandate.

3

Who Made Arabs Refugees?

Who created the Arab refugee problem?

The Arabs themselves.

How?

By rejecting the 1947 United Nations Partition Plan, which offered the Arabs as well as the Jews a permanent sovereign state in Palestine.

What caused thousands of Arabs to flee into adjacent Arab countries and become refugees?

The unexpected Israeli rout of the Arab armies of Egypt, Syria, Jordan, Iraq, Saudi Arabia, and Lebanon, who had invaded Israel following the declaration of independence of Israel by David Ben-Gurion and his cabinet on May 14, 1948.

Were the Arabs forced to leave Israel when the new state was established?

In preparation for the invasion of the Arab armies into Israel, "the Arab League issued orders exhorting the people to seek temporary refuge in neighboring countries, later to return to their abodes in the wake of the victorious Arab armies and obtain their share of the abandoned Jewish property."* Those Arabs who left their homes in the Jewish state did so of their own free will at the urging of their leaders and at the instigation of neighboring Arab governments.†

Did the Israelis try to stop the Arabs from leaving the country?

On April 28, 1948, the Haifa Workers' Council, a branch of Histadrut (Israel's labor federation) distributed posters with an appeal in Arabic and Hebrew:

> Do not fear! Do not destroy your homes with your own hands; do not block off your sources of livelihood; and do not bring upon yourself tragedy by unnecessary evacuation or self-imposed burdens. By moving out you will be overtaken by poverty and humiliation. But in this city, yours and ours, Haifa, the gates are open for work, for life, and for peace, for you and your families.

What was the British view of the Arab exodus?

The British mandatory authorities, about to leave Palestine, conceded that it was not the Jews who had driven the Arabs from their homes. "Every effort is being made by the Jews to persuade the Arab populace to stay and carry on with their normal lives, to get their shops and businesses open and to be assured that their lives and interests will be safe," A.J. Bridmead, Haifa's British Chief of Police, reported on April 26, 1948.

---

*The Research Group for European Migration Problems—REMP Bulletin of January/March 1957.
†See Appendix Note 4.

How did the exodus of the Arabs begin?

The Arab exodus began with the departure of affluent Arabs who preferred to wait out the war in Cairo and Beirut:

> First the wealthiest families went; it was estimated that 20,000 of them left the country in the first two months of internal hostilities. By the end of January, the exodus was already so alarming that the Palestine Arab Higher Committee in alarm asked neighboring Arab countries to refuse visas to these refugees and to seal the borders against them.*

From what city in Israel did the greatest mass exodus take place?

The greatest number left Haifa, where Jews and Arabs had lived in harmony, sharing responsibility for the municipal government. Of the 62,000 Arabs who formerly lived in Haifa, not more than 5,000 or 6,500 remained. On October 2, 1948, the *London Economist* carried a British eyewitness account: "The Jewish authorities urged all Arabs to remain in Haifa and guaranteed them protection and security."

What most influenced the Arabs to leave?

> The announcements made over the air by the Arab Higher Executive, urging all Arabs in Haifa to quit. The reason given was that upon the final withdrawal of the British, the combined armies of the Arab states would invade Palestine and "drive the Jews into the sea," and it was clearly intimated that those Arabs who remained in Haifa and accepted Jewish protection would be regarded as renegades.†

---

*I.F. Stone, *This Is Israel*, Boni & Gaer, New York, New York, 1948.
†*London Economist*, October 2, 1948.

To what countries did the Arab refugees flee?

Many of the people from the north of Palestine emigrated into Syria and Lebanon, most of the people of the south left for Egypt and the Gaza Strip, and most of those who lived in the center left for the remaining parts of Palestine and over to the eastern side of the Jordan. (See map p. 46.)

Why did they choose to go to those countries?

A memorandum of the Arab Higher Committee for Palestine states:

> It was natural for those Palestinian Arabs who felt impelled to leave their country to take refuge in Arab lands near their own ... in order to maintain contact with their country so that it would be easy to return. ... Many were of the opinion that such an opportunity would come "in the hours between sunset and sunrise.*

How many Arab refugees fled what is now Israel?

Figures differ on the precise number of Arabs who left during 1948. The United Nations Economic Survey (Clapp) Mission (1949) estimated the total at about 774,000.

How were they received in the Arab states?

The Arab leaders refused to accept any responsibility for this influx of refugees and permitted them only to settle on arid strips of land without sustenance.

---

*Memorandum of the Arab Higher Committee for Palestine, "The Problem of the Arab Refugees" (Cairo, 1952).

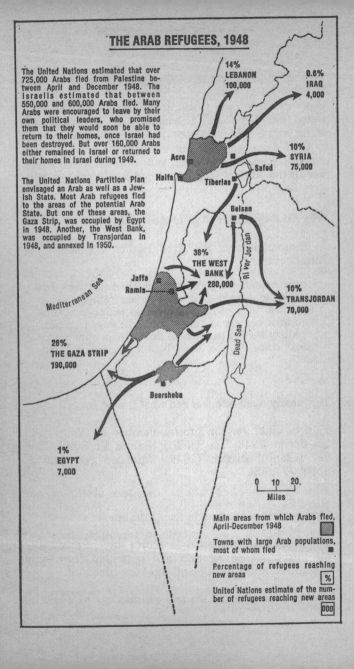

THE ARAB REFUGEES, 1948

The United Nations estimated that over 725,000 Arabs fled from Palestine between April and December 1948. The Israelis estimated that between 550,000 and 600,000 Arabs fled. Many Arabs were encouraged to leave by their own political leaders, who promised them that they would soon be able to return to their homes, once Israel had been destroyed. But over 160,000 Arabs either remained in Israel or returned to their homes in Israel during 1949.

The United Nations Partition Plan envisaged an Arab as well as a Jewish State. Most Arab refugees fled to the areas of the potential Arab State. But one of these areas, the Gaza Strip, was occupied by Egypt in 1948. Another, the West Bank, was occupied by Transjordan in 1948, and annexed in 1950.

14%
LEBANON
100,000

0.6%
IRAQ
4,000

10%
SYRIA
75,000

Acre

Safed

Haifa

Tiberias

Beisan

38%
THE WEST BANK
280,000

Riv ver Jordan

10%
TRANSJORDAN
70,000

Jaffa
Ramla

Mediterranean Sea

26%
THE GAZA STRIP
190,000

Dead Sea

Beersheba

1%
EGYPT
7,000

0   10   20.
Miles

Main areas from which Arabs fled, April-December 1948

Towns with large Arab populations, most of whom fled

Percentage of refugees reaching new areas   %

United Nations estimate of the number of refugees reaching new areas   000

Was citizenship granted the refugees by the Arab "host" nations?

Only Jordan gave them the status of Jordanian citizens and provided them with Jordanian passports.

How have the Arab governments treated these refugees since 1948?

All the governments—Syria, Egypt, Lebanon and Jordan—have kept them in squalid refugee camps, isolated from Arab society. Thousands of men, women, and children, many born long after the establishment of Israel, continue to subsist in the refugee camps as charges of an international body—UNRWA—supported principally by the United States.

Have all of the refugees remained in the camps?

The better-educated and -trained Arabs left the camps to take jobs and become productive citizens in neighboring Arab countries.* More than 600,000 Palestinians still live in 63 refugee camps: 216,245 in Jordan, 54,956 in Syria, 102,136 in Lebanon, 74,941 in the occupied West Bank, and 201,960 in the Gaza Strip.

How have these ex-Palestine refugees aided the oil-rich Persian Gulf countries?

In the sheikdoms of the Arabian peninsula, they have found a ready welcome for their business know-how and have helped in the economic boom of Saudi

---

*In Beirut and Amman, I met teachers, doctors, businessmen, civil servants and technicians who were playing a vital role in the political and economic life of much of the Arab world.

Arabia, Kuwait, Qatar, and Abu Dhabi. In recognition of their contributions, Palestinians have been granted special privileges and enjoy a place close to the sources of power. In Saudi Arabia many of the key people around the Saudi crown prince and the strongman of the regime—Prince Fahd—are Palestinians.

After the 1967 War, was there another flight of Arab refugees?

About 100,000 Arabs fled during and after the fighting, across from the West Bank to the East Bank of the Jordan River and moved into Amman and its environs. On July 2 the Israeli cabinet announced that the refugees who had crossed into Jordan would be allowed to return to Israel. The Israeli government also decided to allow any of the 315,000 Gaza refugees to move to the West Bank, where many of them had relatives.

What other refugee problem was created by the 1948 War?

In addition to the Arab exodus from Israel, more than 500,000 Jewish refugees were forced to flee from their homes in Arab states. During the 1947 United Nations debates, Arab leaders voiced their threats against Jewish citizens in their countries. Egypt announced to the General Assembly: "The lives of a million Jews in Moslem countries will be jeopardized by the establishment of the Jewish state."

Restrictions of movement, riots and pogroms, mass arrests, and confiscation of Jewish property took place in Arab lands.

How many Jews fled these countries to Israel between 1948 and 1967?

567,654 Jews. From Aden—3,912; Algeria—13,119; Egypt—37,867; Iraq—124,647; Lebanon—4,000; Libya—34,265; Morocco—252,642; Syria—4,500; Tunisia—46,255; and Yemen—46,447. (See map p. 50.)

Why is so little heard about these Jewish "refugees," in contrast to the Arab refugees?

Because they never became refugees. They found an open door into Israel and became citizens. The Law of Return, passed by the Israeli parliament in 1950, provides that "every Jew has the right to come to this country as an immigrant . . . who has expressed his desire to settle in Israel."*

What were the conditions under which the Jews left the Arab countries to go to Israel?

Many who had family roots in these Arab countries for centuries were forced to abandon all their property and leave. The Arab governments confiscated all the assets of the former Jewish communities. The total of Jewish property left behind has been estimated at $4 billion to $5 billion.

---

*This article of faith has been observed to the letter in the years since the law was passed with the admission of Jews from eighty-four states. It also includes Arabs and Druzes of Israeli birth.

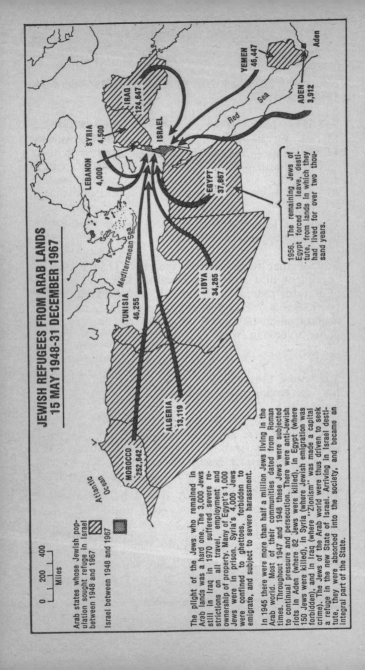

JEWISH REFUGEES FROM ARAB LANDS
15 MAY 1948-31 DECEMBER 1967

0   200   400
Miles

Arab states whose Jewish population sought refuge in Israel between 1948 and 1967

Israel between 1948 and 1967

Atlantic Ocean

MOROCCO 252,642

ALGERIA 13,119

TUNISIA 46,255

Mediterranean Sea

LIBYA 34,265

EGYPT 37,867

LEBANON 4,000

SYRIA 4,500

IRAQ 124,647

ISRAEL

YEMEN 46,447

Red Sea

ADEN 3,912

Aden

1956. The remaining Jews of Egypt forced to leave, destitute, from lands in which they had lived for over two thousand years.

The plight of the Jews who remained in Arab lands was a hard one. The 3,000 Jews still in Iraq in 1970 suffered severe restrictions on all travel, employment and ownership of property. Many of Egypt's 1,000 Jews were in prison. Syria's 4,000 Jews were confined to ghettoes, forbidden to emigrate, and subject to severe harassment.

In 1945 there were more than half a million Jews living in the Arab world. Most of their communities dated from Roman times. Throughout 1947 and 1948 these Jews were subjected to continual pressure and persecution. There were anti-Jewish riots in Aden (where 82 Jews were killed), in Egypt (where Jewish emigration was forbidden), in Syria (where 150 Jews were killed), and in Iraq (where "Zionism" was made a capital crime). The Jews of the Arab world were thus driven to seek a refuge in the new State of Israel. Arriving in Israel destitute, they were absorbed into the society, and became an integral part of the State.

Did the United Nations attempt to solve the Arab refugee problem?

The United Nations set up a commission* on December 11, 1948 which permitted "the refugees wishing to return to their homes and live at peace with their neighbors . . . to do so at the earliest practicable date." It stated that compensation should be paid for the property of those choosing not to return, and that a settlement should be arrived at by direct negotiations. Behind this was the expectation that a quick solution of the refugee problem would be found in the context of a peace settlement.

What was the Arab reaction to the United Nations resolution?

The Arab bloc in the United Nations voted against the resolution. Since then the Arabs have interpreted the resolution as a demand for the unconditional wholesale readmission of the Arab refugees into Israel, and insist that they cannot make peace with Israel unless she opens her doors to all the Arab refugees "wishing to return." The words in the same sentence which specify that the refugees wishing to return to Israel must also want to "live in peace with their neighbors" are ignored.

What did Arab leaders say would be the result if Israel readmitted the Arab refugees?

"If the Arab refugees return to Israel," President Nasser declared to the *Zuricher Woche,* a Swiss newspaper, on September 1, 1961, "Israel will cease to exist." "It is obvious," the official Egyptian radio commented

*The United Nations Palestine Conciliation Commission, General Assembly Resolution 194 (II).

on September 13, 1961, "that the return of one million Arabs to Palestine will make them the majority of Israel's inhabitants. They will then be able to impose their will on the Jews and expel them from Palestine."

Did Israel attempt to comply with the United Nations resolution calling for negotiations on the refugee problem?

On May 5, 1949 Foreign Minister Abba Eban made the following statement in the United Nations: "Our first objective . . . will be to reach an agreement by direct negotiations on the contribution to be made by each Government towards the settlement of this grave problem." The Arabs turned down the offer and have done so repeatedly ever since.

Has Israel agreed to pay compensation to the Arab refugees?

Ever since 1949, from the rostrum of the United Nations and on many other occasions, Israel has expressed her willingness to compensate Arab refugees for lands and property abandoned in Israel.* The Arab countries have spurned these offers and demanded immediate repatriation of the refugees as part of any deal. The Israelis maintain that any negotiations regarding compensation by them would have to take into account the claims for the property which 500,000 Israel citizens had abandoned in various Arab countries which had been confiscated by them.

---

*On May 5, 1949 Israel Foreign Minister Abba Eban told the General Assembly of the United Nations: "The government of Israel has already announced its acceptance of obligations to make compensation for lands abandoned."

What has Israel done to financially assist the Arab refugees?

Since 1952 Israel has unconditionally released Arab refugee bank accounts in Israel amounting to $10,-000,000. The Arab governments had forbidden the refugees to request the release of their accounts from Israel and had even imprisoned refugees for being in contact with the enemy for that purpose.

What plans have been offered to Arab countries to solve their refugee problem?

Dag Hammarskjold, the late Secretary-General of the United Nations, recommended a large-scale development plan for the Middle East which would have brought about a far-reaching transformation of this underdeveloped area and would have permitted the absorption of large numbers of refugees.* The Arab countries have rejected all plans, including two that this writer made for the State Department, which would have provided an improvement for the condition of the refugees and especially their integration into the host countries.

Has the problem of the Arab refugees been blown out of proportion?

There have been tens of millions of persons displaced due to the wars of this century, mostly resolved by *resettlement* rather than repatriation.†

---

*A report of the Clapp Mission called for the gradual assimilation of the refugees in the economy of the area.

†As compared with the approximate 1,000,000 Arab refugees, there were 13,000,000 Germans who were forced to flee from the Soviet armies and her satellites, over 50,000,000 refugees on the Indian subcontinent, 8,000,000 refugees in East Pakistan, and approximately 2,000,000 refugees from North Vietnam. In each case, these mass dislocations were followed by constructive emergency measures of the war-torn nations and international agencies in time to avert new explosions, to bind the wounds of the victims, and build the uprooted populations into revitalized new societies.

What action did the United Nations take to assist with a solution to the refugee problem?

It established, through a resolution of the General Assembly on December 8, 1949, UNRWA (United Nations Relief and Works Administration)—an agency to provide relief and work for Palestine refugees.

4

The UNRWA Scandal

Which agency of the United Nations helps finance terrorism?

UNRWA.

How?

By servicing the refugees in barren camps established for rehabilitation and temporary relief but turned into arsenals by terrorists for training and military operations.

Did UNRWA camps serve as key military centers in the violent civil war in Lebanon?

Yes. The crucial battles of the bloody hostilities raged around Tal Zaatar and Jisr el-Basha camps which housed 25,000 Palestinians and 30,000 Lebanese refugees on the southeast side of Beirut. The Palestinians (PLO) and leftist Moslem forces battled the Maronite Christians supported by the Syrians for control of Tal Zaatar, a bastion which the Christian militants finally captured after 52 days of siege.

Who has been the major financial supporter of the UNRWA refugees in the camps in the Middle East?

The U.S. taxpayer. Since its inception more than 26 years ago, the United States has contributed 62 percent ($645,964,592) of the approximate $1 billion toward the total upkeep of the UNRWA operation.* The United States contribution for 1976 was $38,700,000.

Who runs the UNRWA organization?

Approximately 15,600 employees, mostly Arabs who are themselves on the "refugee" roles. There are also 126 American and European officials who operate in the organization's central headquarters in Beirut. Financial control and policy is directed from the UNRWA office at the United Nations in New York.

How many Arab refugees† were there originally?

The figures have been subject to considerable debate. From the outset almost overnight they began to mount. On August 2, 1948, Sir Alexander Cadogan, the British delegate, told the United Nations Security

---

*Besides the U.S. contribution, Great Britain has provided 14 percent of the total. The balance has been made up of small offerings from other Western countries. The Soviet Union and the Eastern-bloc nations provided nothing. Israel has contributed more than $6,000,000. The Arab "host" countries (Egypt, Jordan, Lebanon and Syria) have from time to time made minuscule token gifts ranging from 1 percent to 2 percent. Only in recent years have the Arab oil producers made any substantial contribution, which in 1975 was less than 12 percent of the total.

†A Palestine refugee, as defined by the UNRWA report of July 1, 1974 to June 30, 1975, "is a person whose normal residence was Palestine for a minimum of two years preceding the conflict in 1948 and who, as a result of this conflict, lost both his home and means of livelihood and took refuge, in 1948, in one of the countries where UNRWA provides relief. Refugees within this definition or the children or grandchildren of such refugees are eligible for Agency assistance if they are (a) registered with UNRWA, (b) living in the area of UNRWA's operations, and (c) in need."

Council that there "are no less than 250,000 Arab refugees from Palestine." The statistics were inflated late that August. Abdul Azzam Pasha, Secretary General of the Arab League, raised the figure to 582,248. Count Folke Bernadotte, the United Nations mediator, stated on September 16, 1948 that "there are approximately 330,000 Arab refugees from Palestine." One month later, on October 18, 1948, Ralph Bunche, who became acting mediator after Bernadotte's assassination, put the number of Arab refugees at 472,000. In June 1949 the United Nations was informed that there were 711,000 Arab refugees; in June 1951 they were put at 879,667. By 1969 the reports of UNRWA placed the number of Arab refugees at 1,300,000.

How many refugees are there now?

There were 1,668,205* Palestinians still registered with UNRWA according to the 1975 UNRWA report. They include the refugees living both inside and outside the camps who nevertheless receive the same services from UNRWA—schools, rations, health clinics. Those who live outside the camps move freely in adjacent areas, many securing funds from employment in addition to the rations from UNRWA. A number of them have found jobs in building, industry, and transportation, and others have found work in the Gulf states and particularly in Saudi Arabia.

What are the supplies that UNRWA provides?

Monthly rations consisting of flour, sugar, rice, and cooking oil. Also provided are kerosene, soap, clothing, blankets, and shoes.

---

*The total number of refugees inside the UNRWA camps is 651,736. The refugees outside the camps number 1,016,469. There are 644,669 refugees in Jordan, 296,628 in the occupied West Bank, 339,824 in the Gaza Strip, 198,637 in Lebanon, and 188,447 in Syria.

How many rations are said to be provided by UNRWA for each refugee?

The UNRWA report for 1975 states that "the ration provides approximately 1,500 calories per day" in summer and "1,600 calories per day" in winter.

Do the refugees actually live on these limited rations?

The fact is that virtually *no* one lives on the rations meted out by UNRWA. The rations are delivered in trucks and usually immediately reloaded onto other trucks by entrepreneurs who buy them from refugee ration-card holders for pittances. They are not distributed to the refugees.

How do the refugees obtain their increased food supplies?

Every refugee camp has shops in which food and other merchandise are sold. There usually are many stalls where fresh vegetables, dairy, and fresh meat may be bought. The marketing is brisk. In many instances, the funds of the refugees derive from remittances received from breadwinners employed in the oil countries. Many hire themselves out during planting and harvesting seasons.*

What caused the growth of UNRWA refugee rolls?

Since there was no tight control for admission to the camps, Arabs other than refugees flocked to them.

---

*In every camp I visited, I would ask the *mukhtar* (mayor) to take me to the poorest family. In no instance did I see any family subsisting on rations. There were always vegetables and milk. UNRWA's reference to rations and calories is distortion.

Though inadequate by Western criteria, the standards of living, housing, nutrition, and education in the camps were far superior to those to which the refugees were accustomed in their homes. Modern medical care provided to the refugees by the United Nations is responsible for the low mortality rate in the camps, a major factor in the growth of the camp population.

Have the UNRWA rolls accurately reflected the actual number of refugees in the camps?

In 1952 UNRWA reported to the U.N. General Assembly: "Whereas all births are eagerly announced [at the camps], the deaths whenever possible are passed over in silence, so that the family may continue to collect rations for the deceased." On July 20, 1955, Henry Labouisse, director of UNRWA said, "There are refugees who hold as many as five hundred UNRWA ration cards, and they are dealing in UNRWA-approved clothing ration cards."*

How did Arab nonrefugees become eligible for UNRWA support?

When the 1948 Israel War of Independence ended, many Arabs living in the territory seized by Jordan, the West Bank and Old Jerusalem, claimed that they were entitled to relief because they had become indigent as a result of the war. Numbers of Arabs who had never lived in the area which became Israel were given the status of refugees by UNRWA. Padding of the UNRWA rolls for rations followed, calling for rectification of the refugee lists.

---

*See Appendix Note 5.

Did UNRWA attempt to take a census to establish the legitimate number of refugees?

Every effort by UNRWA authorities failed because the Jordan and Egyptian "host" governments refused to cooperate.

Was there an urgent need for a full-scale census?

Black-market commerce in ration cards, false names, failure to report deaths and numerous other abuses were distorting and defeating the purpose of the "rescue and *works*" operation designated in the terms of reference by the United Nations. The abuses were becoming common practice; many refugees originally seen as charges of UNRWA were now growing into a "permanent" welfare populace.

How extensive was the black market in refugee ration cards?

UNRWA ration cards became a form of "illegal tender." Commerce in the cards by Arab racketeers reached alarming proportions.*

Has there ever been an accurate census of the number of Arabs in the camps?

Following the victory in June 1967, the Israelis occupied the West Bank of Jordan and the Gaza Strip,

---

*While in Beirut in June 1968, following a visit to every Arab refugee camp for a report to the State Department, this writer witnessed a professional dealer in ration cards doing an active business. Of course, there was the usual haggling over price, but eventually money and ration cards changed hands. These cards, which would seem to represent petty graft since they buy only four cents' worth of food a day—1,500 calories—are actually an important clue to the distortion of Arab refugee statistics. Very often the cards are in the names of persons hundreds of miles away.

where most of the refugees encamped. As the government with authority to organize a census, at the writer's urging, they undertook an independent, full-scale census.

Did the figures from the Israel census differ from those of UNRWA?

An excerpt from the Israeli census report revealed the disparity between their figures and those of UNRWA.*

What opportunities has Israel provided the refugees on the West Bank and Gaza Strip since her occupation following the 1967 War?

Israel invested substantial sums to send special teams to instruct Arab farmers in the use of modern equipment and methods in agriculture. Loans are granted Arabs for the erection of new industrial plants and the extension and improvement of existing ones. Israel has also opened vocational training centers for young Arabs to become skilled workers. By 1972, 40,000 Arab workers traveled from their towns and villages every morning to Israeli building sites and factories. The result has been the reduction of unemployment among the refugees still living in camps, most from the Gaza Strip area, where they had been kept in idleness by the Egyptians.†

Has there been a rise in the standard of living among the Arab refugees on the West Bank and the Gaza Strip?

There has been a sharp rise. The Israeli administration has undertaken a program of thinning out

---

*See Appendix Note 6 for detailed figures.
†See Appendix Note 7.

crowded camps, particularly in the Gaza Strip. Whole new neighborhoods have been built where camp residents can receive vastly improved housing at a nominal cost. New houses include indoor plumbing, electricity, and running water—amenities absent in the refugee camps.

Have the health conditions of the Arabs improved in the occupied territories since Israel has controlled them?

Since 1967 the number of doctors and dentists for the Arabs on the West Bank has doubled, and the number of hospital beds increased 20 percent. Malaria has been stamped out; a sharp drop in deaths from measles and poliomyelitis—factors which have halved the infant mortality rate. The West Bank has more physicians per capita than Jordan, Syria, Iraq, Libya, or Saudi Arabia.

What percentage of the total annual UNRWA budget is used for education?

In 1975* expenditure on education and training amounted to $50.8 million and accounted for 45.4 percent of the agency's budget.

Who is responsible for the educational program in the camps?

UNESCO (United Nations Educational, Scientific and Cultural Organization) is charged with the professional aspects of the education of 288,893 (1975–76)* refugees. They draw their funds from the central UNRWA budget.

*Latest available figures.

Where are the teachers in the UNRWA camps drawn from?

The 5,112 teachers are mainly Arab refugees, many in the camps since childhood.

Have the UNRWA teachers used propaganda in their lessons to the Arab children?

Some of the teaching was focussed on hatred of the Jews.*

What are some examples of educational materials used by UNRWA teachers?

The textbooks and propaganda literature were printed and supplied to the teachers by UNESCO from UNRWA funds. Among those I found was the infamous *Protocols of the Learned Elders of Zion,* a notorious forgery circulated in czarist Russia that alleges a Jewish plot to take over the world. A Syrian first-grade reader declares: "The Jews are enemies of Arabs. Soon we will rescue Palestine from their hands." A standard exercise book is decorated with a map of Israel showing a rocket directed at Tel Aviv. Another book, for fourteen-year-olds, asserts: "Israel exists in the heart of the Arab homeland. Its extermination is vital for the preservation of Arabism and the renaissance of the Arabs."

---

*In my investigations accompanied by translators from the American embassy in the UNRWA schools, I heard how the teachers used propaganda against the Jews as part of the children's catechism. The students were being systematically brainwashed and incited to hatred by their teachers, usually themselves refugees who were venting their prejudice against Israel in the classrooms.

What steps have been taken to ban the inflammatory textbooks used for educating refugees in the UNRWA camps?

In April 1969, UNESCO recommended that fourteen Arab textbooks be banned from the U.N.–administered schools in the Middle East because they advocated war on Israel and showed contempt for Jews.* When UNRWA finally took some steps in response to Israeli complaints and stopped buying Syrian textbooks for refugee schools, Syrian Education Minister Souleyman El-Khish complained: "The hatred we indoctrinate into the minds of our youth from birth is sacrosanct. . . . It constitutes one of our instruments for the protection of our homelands and our national heritage."

Are the UNRWA camps used by Palestine terrorist groups in their activities against Israel?

The terrorists have operated freely in the southeastern and southwestern regions of Lebanon and in the refugee camps scattered throughout the country, where the terrorist organizations not only recruit and train but also run the camps (although under the UNRWA operational "umbrella"). In effect, the Arab terrorists control the surrounding Lebanese territory, with the refugee camps and villages becoming extraterritorial enclaves outside of Lebanese government control. Photos have appeared in *The New York Times* and other publications and on TV, showing the terrorists training in refugee camps with youths using automatic weapons, explosives, and guerrilla tactics.

---

*This followed the strong protest in my report to the State Department after my visit to the UNRWA camp-schools.

The fifteen refugee camps in Lebanon have served as military bases for PLO terrorists.*

What was the 1969 Lebanon and PLO agreement?

It was an agreement to coordinate the activities of the PLO in Lebanon. It gave the PLO permission for free movement all over Lebanon. It also entitled the PLO to act freely and obtain assistance from the Lebanese government when the group attacked Israel.

How did the Lebanese government react to the heavy buildup of weapons in the UNRWA camps in Lebanon before the civil war in 1975–76?

In 1974 the Lebanese government became apprehensive when it learned the Palestinians were secretly being armed with weapons considerably more powerful than handguns or rifles. It ordered the Palestinians to surrender the weapons or to move out. The result was a nine-day conflict with hundreds of casualties which ended in a stalemate, leaving the Palestinians heavily armed in Lebanon.

Did any of the UNRWA staff and the refugees serve in the fighting against Israel in the 1967 War?

UNRWA fought in the war, and the UNRWA staff suffered the heaviest casualty rate of any of the belligerents. In the Gaza Strip, where UNRWA had a salaried staff of about 3,500 the casualty rate was probably well above 15 percent. This compares with 1,150 casualties suffered by Ahmed Shukairy's† ir-

---

*In my visits to the camps, I learned firsthand that the terrorist leaders and the Arab governments made no secret of the fact that they were using the camps, when strategically located, as military training centers to prepare for assaults on Israel.

†Former Chairman of the Palestinian National Committee.

regular mercenary UNRWA-supported guerrilla army of 10,000.

Did Shukairy's men receive compensation from any other source?

Yes, they received salaries from Egypt, and the payrolls of the mercenaries were met by cooperation of UNRWA through two Gaza banks, the records of which were seized by the victorious Israeli army. The pay of 14 dinar (about $35) a month was most attractive to men receiving free housing, rations, and care for their families from UNRWA, which then received 70 percent of its budget from the U.S. Treasury.

Have efforts been made to expose the operations of UNRWA in the refugee camps?

The author made two exhaustive surveys and reports of the camps for the U.S. State Department and the United Nations—in January 1963 and again in June 1967, immediately following the Six-Day War. An excerpt from the 1963 report reads:

> Does the American taxpayer know that he is continuing to support a political program set up by Arab feudal leaders to keep refugees in a moribund state—and that the United Nations is serving as an international charity agent so that the lives of a million Arabs have become pitiful pawns?*

During the twenty-seven years of its existence, have efforts been made to phase out or eliminate UNRWA?

A number of recommendations had been made to phase out the operation before it became integrated

---

*See Appendix Note 8 for another excerpt from report of January 1963.

into the Arab communities, but these were sidetracked. Some efforts were made to find work for the refugees in the neighboring Arab "oil" countries but it was aborted. An effort by the author to provide conditions for legitimate labor outside the camps was made in 1960, but failed.*

Where would the refugees live if the camps were disbanded?

They would be absorbed into the life of their "host" countries. In Jordan, where almost 50 percent of the refugees reside, they have become citizens of the state.

Have the UNRWA operations in Lebanon been affected by the country's violent civil war?

UNRWA offices at the United Nations in New York report that the severe upheaval in the Beirut area has caused many of the 160,000 occupants to flee the camps; also that part of UNRWA Headquarters formerly located in Beirut were moved to Amman, Jordan and temporarily to distant Vienna.

---

*In 1960, in a survey for the United States and the United Nations, I visited every Arab refugee camp. A new source of employment for the idle refugees opened up when I learned of the critical need for laborers in the Persian Gulf oil-producing countries, principally Saudi Arabia and Kuwait. Since the refugees were not trained for labor, I helped introduce vocational training schools under UNRWA auspices financed by the U.S. oil companies in the Arab countries for the unskilled refugees to prepare them to work in the oil producing countries. The objective was to provide the refugees with work and compensation which would reduce their dependence on UNRWA rations and diminish the population of the camps. The training and exit of thousands of refugees from the camps to the Arab oil countries succeeded, but it ran into a major unexpected obstacle. The refugees who went to work in Kuwait and Saudi Arabia left their wives and families behind in the refugee camps. Instead of the families' surrendering their UNRWA ration cards, they retained them, thus continuing to draw rations on top of the salaries that their husbands sent to their "homes" in the camps.

Why was UNRWA's original purpose distorted?

The perpetuation of the life of UNRWA from its originally intended temporary humanitarian purpose to twenty-seven years' duration (and beyond) was bound to weaken and distort its original purpose. The Arab leaders exploited UNRWA by manipulating the destitute refugees for their own political objectives and transforming many of the camps into military arsenals.

What should now be a practical solution to the problem of UNRWA?

With the UNRWA camps having served as the staging centers for the Lebanon onslaughts, there can be no further justification for the continuation of these camps. The United States should discontinue its support and insist on the dispersal of the refugees as soon as possible into the countries of their "brothers" to which they had fled twenty-eight years ago. American policy should now be directed toward persuading the rich oil states of the Persian Gulf to foot the bill of resettling the Palestinian refugees within the Arab world. The elimination of the refugee camps would remove the sites from which the PLO can operate and would put a brake on their remaining military effectiveness. It would also transfer the education of the refugee children from an international body to the Arab countries where the responsibility belongs.

5

The Specter of International Terrorism

What aspect of the Arab-Israeli conflict most directly threatens us all?

We are all threatened by the escalating spread of Arab terrorism and the extreme physical danger it poses to innocent people all over the world.

Which Arab terrorist act has drawn the greatest worldwide attention?

The hijacking, on June 27, 1976, of an Air France jetliner with 257 people aboard, by Palestinian and pro-Palestinian terrorists.

Why did this particular hijacking receive so much attention?

Because of the large number of hostages who were known to be in great jeopardy—the 103 who were not released; because of the direct complicity of the Ugandan government; but primarily because of the Israelis' daring and successful Fourth of July rescue of the hostages at Entebbe Airport.

When referring to such acts, the news media interchangably use the terms "terrorist," "guerrilla," "commando"—which is accurate?

By accepted definition, it is *terrorism* being practiced by the Palestinian organizations which have been guilty of attacks on Israeli citizens and reckless disregard for uninvolved bystanders since 1948.

What specifically characterizes these acts as terrorism?

They are *intentionally* (not *accidentally,* as is supposed to be the case in air raids) directed against civilian populations. Senator Daniel Moynihan, defines the main principle of terrorism as showing no distinction between soldiers and civilians as targets of armed assaults. "For the terrorists there are no innocent bystanders."*

These Palestinian organizations say they are at war with Israel. Doesn't this justify their claim to being guerrillas?

Guerrillas such as the partisans and underground resistance groups of World War II fame planned their operations against German troops and military installations. They did not try to infiltrate into Germany to kill civilians, as the Palestinians do in Israel. The accepted role of guerrilla requires that he abide by universally accepted codes of warfare which distinguish between combatants and noncombatants.

*New York Magazine, July 26, 1976.

Are the Palestinian hijackers and infiltrators commandos?

Commando refers to those units of a regular military organization which perform special missions usually behind enemy lines; sometimes as part of a larger military operation or, as is most often the case, as the main components of a surprise raid on an enemy position. Commandos do not operate against innocent civilians. The Israeli rescue mission at Entebbe Airport clearly showed the distinction between commandos and terrorists. The Israelis were the commandos; the Palestinians were the terrorists.

Which are the major Palestinian terrorist organizations?

The Black September Group of Al Fatah, named to commemorate the PLO expulsion from Jordan in September 1970, was formed in 1971 by Saleh Khalek, Yasir Arafat's second-in-command. It counts among its exploits the assassination of Jordan's Prime Minister Wafsi Tal in 1971, the murder of eleven Israeli athletes at the 1972 Munich Olympics, the murder of the American ambassador to Sudan and two other diplomats in Khartoum in 1973, and numerous kidnapping and killing attacks within Israel.

The Popular Front for the Liberation of Palestine is a Marxist group which split off from the PLO in the late 1960s, specializes in spectacular acts of international terrorism such as aircraft hijackings. It is believed to have 1,000 potential action and support agents in the Middle East and Europe, and maintains close links with other extreme left-wing groups such as the Japanese Red Army, with whom it cooperated in the Lod Airport massacre of 26 tourists (and the wounding of 78) at Tel Aviv in 1972. It also staged the hijacking of the Air France jetliner in June 1976, using members of the German Baader-Meinhof gang, who were among the terrorists killed in the Israeli rescue operation at Entebbe. The leader of the PFLP is Dr. George Habash, a Lebanese Christian, and its operations commander is Dr. Wadi Haddad, a Palestinian.

How many aircraft hijackings were committed by Palestinian terrorists?

Since 1968, the beginning of the peak era of hijacking, over 30 were attributed to Palestinian or pro-Palestinian terrorists, plus 3 airport massacres. Only 11 hijacking attempts have been foiled. The human cost has been heavy: 201 have been killed, 213 injured.*

Who provides arms and training for terrorist organizations?

Libya's leader Colonel Qaddafi has been supplying arms to Moslem terrorist organizations in the Middle East, Africa, Asia (and has even supplied Soviet-made arms to the Irish Republican Army in Northern Ireland.) Libya serves as the main training center for international terrorists in the Middle East, where they are supplied with forged passports, cash, documents, contracts, and weapons. The terrorists who murdered the Israeli athletes at the Olympic games in Munich in 1972 had been trained in Libya and had their arms smuggled into Munich by Libyan diplomatic couriers.

Where do countries like Libya buy the kind of weapons terrorists require?

The basic weapons such as machine guns as well as sophisticated hand-held rocket launchers used by

---

*See Appendix Note 9.

terrorists to shoot down civilian aircraft are supplied by the Soviet Union.

Are Palestinian terrorists liable to severe penalties for their acts?

Only in Israel are they certain of long imprisonment. Arab countries usually free them outright (sometimes even rewarding them) or give them their liberty under the guise of "house arrest" sentences. Other governments, including those of Western Europe, either fail to prosecute Palestinian terrorists or let them off with light sentences in deference to the oil-producing Arab nations. For those terrorists caught and tried, the average sentence (Israel excluded) has been only 18 months. Of the 267 international terrorists, including Palestinians, apprehended since 1970, less than half were still in jail as of September 1975. The terrorists pay a high price in casualties and prisoners. Between the Six-Day War and December 31, 1971, the Israelis imprisoned more than 5,000 Palestinians captured in raids or sentenced for terrorist activities.

Besides light sentences, what other guarantee do the terrorists have of escaping punishment?

In recent years, terrorist recruits have been told by their leaders that if they are captured alive, a subsequent terrorist action will gain them freedom through exchange for hostages.

What is today's terrorist like?

The contemporary terrorist is a full-time professional who takes part in a well-planned and usually highly co-ordinated operation. Intelligence specialists of concerned governments estimate that there are at least 200 full-time terrorists operating in Europe and the

Middle East, plus thousands of potential "action agents," mostly Palestinians, who can be recruited for single operations. Terrorist organizations are usually composed of people who have decided that they alone shall decree how their particular society shall be composed and how it shall function, and are prepared to spare no one in their attempts to force all existing authority to yield to them.

In what way has terrorism become "international"?

To the extent that terrorist groups that previously operated separately, with no outside contacts, now cooperate and coordinate their operations. Even though their motives may differ, from the creation of a Palestinian state to traditional European anarchism, they now help plan and participate in each other's operations.

What is an example of an international terrorist operation?

The June 1976 hijacking of the Air France jetliner was carried out by German terrorists associated with the Baader-Meinhof gang and by Palestinian terrorists. Their headquarters for this operation was in Somalia, the Soviet Union's strategic ally in Africa. One of the sponsors of this terrorist act was Libya, which supplies hundreds of millions of dollars of its oil revenues for the training and equipping of terrorists, and which provided the refueling stop for the hijacked aircraft on its way to its preplanned destination, the Ugandan airfield at Entebbe. At Entebbe the Ugandan government furnished additional equipment and assistance to the hijackers and the terrorists who arrived from Somalia according to the prearranged plan. This terrorist operation had involved three African countries, at least two—Uganda and Libya—in direct complicity, and agents of terrorist organizations from Europe and the Arab Middle East.

What is the ultimate goal of the Palestine terrorist organizations?

Their ultimate goal is the elimination of the State of Israel and its replacement with a Palestinian state according to their own design.

What is the Palestinians' rationale for the use of terrorism?

Al Fatah's monthly publication, *The Palestinian Revolution* (June 1968, page 38), describes it:

> The aim of this war is not to impose our will on the enemy but to destroy him in order to take his place. ... In a conventional war there is no need to continue the war if the enemy submits to our will ... while in a people's war there is no deterrent inhibition, for its aim is not to defeat the enemy but to exterminate him.

Have the Palestinian terrorist organizations always used international terrorism as a method to achieve their ends?

Beginning in the early 1950s, terrorist activities against Israel were highly localized, clandestine raids for the purpose of killing civilians or sabotaging vital installations. International terrorism directed against Israel is a recent development, and although the overall Palestinian objectives remain the same, the means used including worldwide publicity add a new dimension to the old method of direct terrorism aimed at the Israeli population to force them to submit.

How do the Palestinians hope to achieve their objectives through international terrorism?

By enlarging their field of operations to virtually the whole world, they achieve the maximum exposure and attention for their cause; and by revealing to this new large audience the extremes to which they are prepared to go in their cause, they hope to convince this audience of the seriousness of the Palestinian grievances and possibly enlist sympathy and support. When the terrorist violence was localized at the borders of Israel, the rest of the world was unaffected; but international terrorism threatens everyone, and the Palestinians may be hoping that public opinion will agree with their contention that eliminating the cause of the terrorism—the State of Israel—may ultimately be the only way of ending the threat of it.

Why did the Palestinian terrorists decide to put greater emphasis on acts such as hijacking?

Many of the Palestinian terrorists have been educated in European universities and had absorbed the techniques of civil protest and media manipulation that are enhanced by spectacular acts such as aircraft hijacking. Zehdi Labib Terzi, the PLO's chief observer at the United Nations puts it this way: "The first several hijackings aroused the consciousness of the world to our cause and awakened the media and world opinion much more—and more effectively—than twenty years of pleading at the United Nations."

Did the hijacking of the Air France jetliner to Entebbe help the Palestinian cause?

As spectacular as the hijacking was, it was totally overshadowed by the even more spectacular Israeli rescue. As an exploit to dramatize the Palestinian cause, it backfired by dramatizing instead the Israeli determination not to submit to terrorism. However, the heroics of the Israeli rescue should not obscure the intention of the Arab act of terrorism.

Is international terrorism expected to end if the Palestinians should succeed in causing Israel's downfall?

If terrorism succeeds against Israel, it will be used against other established democracies, according to Senator Daniel Moynihan. "Israel has become the metaphor for democracy as . . . attacks by terrorists on Israeli civilians has become a metaphor for the general assault on democracy and decency. . . ."*

What direction will terrorism take if the Palestinians fail to achieve their political goals?

Terrorists will probably escalate the frequency and intensity of their activities to hold world attention.† Professor Irving Howe, political analyst explains: "Terrorists are driven to greater, more extreme violence to force the press and the world to pay attention." Even more disturbing is this prediction by a CIA deputy director: "Terrorism will get worse and may even involve the use of nuclear devices." Terrorists could steal enough nuclear materials to make their own bombs and ". . . hold a whole city hostage to achieve their goals."

---

*From a speech delivered at Hebrew University, Jerusalem, at the time of the Entebbe rescue.

†An example of this is the machine-gun and hand-grenade attack on August 12, 1976, soon after the Entebbe rescue, in Istanbul's Yasilkov Airport on passengers who were about to board a Tel Aviv-bound El Al plane, in which 3 persons were killed and 24 injured. The terrorists were members of the Popular Front for the Liberation of Palestine, the same organization which was responsible for the Entebbe hijacking. The 2 captured terrorists stated that their mission was to "kill as many Israelis as we can."

Has Arab terrorism succeeded as a means of achieving its political objectives?

Its program of assault and bloodshed calculated to destroy Israel as a state has failed abysmally.

What is the possible solution to combat international terrorism?

If the free countries of the world would agree that they would boycott any country involved with hijacking or terrorism, and, according to Chaim Herzog, Israeli ambassador to the United Nations, if that country "knows that it will be cut off entirely from the world if it harbors terrorists and hijackers . . . there will be no more hijacking."

Are there any examples of the powers of the West acting to oppose terrorism when tested?

The evidence is negative. On January 11, 1977 a French court freed Abu Daoud, who is known to have commanded the slaying of Israeli athletes at the 1972 Munich Olympics, and without a trial gave him a free first-class ticket to Algeria. The West German government, which along with Israel had requested Daoud's extradition, stated that his release makes the "fight against international terrorism" more difficult. World opinion reacted against the French for playing into the hands of the terrorists.

Is there any action against terrorism being taken by the nations of the world?

The first U.N. globally sponsored measure against terrorism, advanced by West Germany and 37 other nations, is assured passage in the General Assembly. This rare U.N. unanimity, which includes Arab states as well as the Soviet Union, is a step toward recognition of the necessity for eliminating the blight of terrorism from the world's landscape.

6

PLO Exposed

What was the first Palestinian terrorist organization against the established state of Israel?

In the early 1950s a group of Palestinian students studying in Cairo including Yasir Arafat, were encouraged by the Egyptian government to form the General Union of Palestine Students. Secretly trained by Egyptian military personnel for occasional *fedayin* guerrilla raids from the Gaza Strip on settlements inside Israel,* they operated until the Suez crisis in 1956, and were disbanded when the first U.N. force was stationed in Sinai to patrol the Israeli-Egyptian border. (See map p. 81.)

Which is the oldest terrorist organization operating against Israel?

Al Fatah. Organized in Kuwait in 1959 by Yasir Arafat, its official name is the Palestine Liberation Movement. In Arabic the initials of the name are HTF, producing the acronym "hataf," the Arabic word for "death." Considered inappropriate for an

---

*At the author's first meeting with President Nasser in his home in Heliopolis, a suburb of Cairo in 1955, the Egyptian leader expressed deep concern over Israel's attacks in Gaza on Fatah bases and the reprisals his army leaders were demanding that he take.

TERRORIST RAIDS INTO ISRAEL
1951-1956

Palestinian terrorist groups, or Fedayeen, began systematic raids into Israel from 1950. Towards the end of 1954, the Egyptian Government supervised the formal establishment of Palestinian terrorist groups in the Gaza strip and north-eastern Sinai. Throughout 1955 an increasing number of raids were launched into Israel. From 1951 to 1956, Israeli vehicles were ambushed, farms attacked, fields booby trapped and roads mined. Fedayeen from Gaza also infiltrated into Jordan, and operated from there. Saudi Arabia, Syria and Lebanon each gave the Fedayeen support and refuge. Local Jordanian-Palestinian Fedayeen were also active operating from the West Bank.

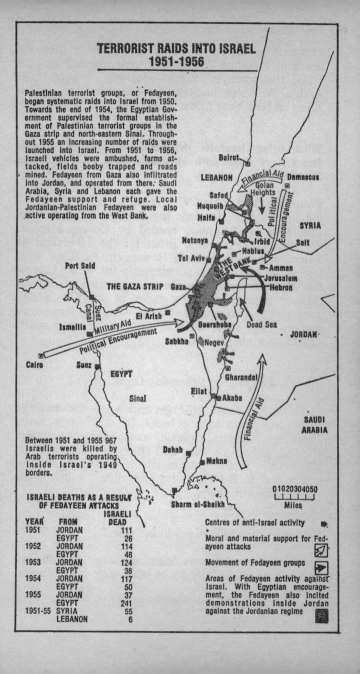

Between 1951 and 1955 967 Israelis were killed by Arab terrorists operating inside Israel's 1949 borders.

ISRAELI DEATHS AS A RESULT OF FEDAYEEN ATTACKS

YEAR	FROM	ISRAELI DEAD
1951	JORDAN	111
	EGYPT	26
1952	JORDAN	114
	EGYPT	48
1953	JORDAN	124
	EGYPT	38
1954	JORDAN	117
	EGYPT	50
1955	JORDAN	37
	EGYPT	241
1951-55	SYRIA	55
	LEBANON	6

Centres of anti-Israel activity

Moral and material support for Fedayeen attacks

Movement of Fedayeen groups

Areas of Fedayeen activity against Israel. With Egyptian encouragement, the Fedayeen also incited demonstrations inside Jordan against the Jordanian regime

0 10 20 30 40 50
Miles

organization dedicated to the return rather than the death of Palestine, the initials were reversed to read FTH, the acronym "fatah" meaning "conquest" in Arabic. Al Fatah launched its first operation against Israel on New Year's Day 1965.*

What other terrorist organizations directed against Israel have come into existence since Al Fatah was formed?

Following the Six-Day War in June 1967, the following groups were formed: the Popular Front for the Liberation of Palestine, headed by George Habash; the Popular Democratic Front for the Liberation of Palestine, headed by Na'if Hawatmeh; As Saiqa, controlled by the Syrian government; the Arab Liberation Front, controlled by the Iraqi government. Several splinter groups, including those of the Communist parties of Jordan, Iraq, and Syria were also formed, so that by 1969 there were at least six known terrorist organizations in the field.

What is the Palestine Liberation Organization?

PLO is the umbrella organization of the terrorist groups operating against Israel. Its main body is the Palestine National Council, comprised of delegates from all guerrilla groups and other Palestine exile organizations. Power rests mainly in the Central Committee and in the Executive Committee, which Yasir Arafat currently chairs.

How does the PLO finance its activities?

Most Arab governments contribute directly to the organization, particularly those with large oil revenues.

---

*The only casualty of this operation was an Arab guerrilla who was wounded by a Jordanian border guard.

In addition, Palestinians living in Arab countries contribute voluntarily to the PLO, or through a so-called "liberation tax" levied by the Arab governments for the PLO.

How did the PLO originate?

The Egyptian, Syrian and Iraqi governments had introduced the idea of "the Palestinian entity" in Arab League meetings since 1959. In May 1964 the first National Palestinian Congress attended by 388 delegates from Palestinian exile committees in several Arab countries met in East Jerusalem (Jordan) and founded the Palestine Liberation Organization. Its Secretary-General was Ahmed Shukairy, a Palestinian politician who declared the PLO's intention to "drive the Jews [of Israel] into the sea." The PLO created a bureaucratic structure for Palestine-in-Exile, but the organization was actually controlled by the established Arab governments.

How did Yasir Arafat gain control of the PLO?

After the results of the 1967 Six-Day War, the Palestinians in the newly occupied territories as well as those in Arab countries, looked for a new leader to replace the discredited PLO leadership. They found him in Yasir Arafat, whose Al Fatah had been staging occasional forays on Israeli settlements from Jordan. In 1968 Arafat took over the leadership of the PLO, and Al Fatah became the dominant group in the organization.

What kind of political action against Israel has the PLO engaged in?

The PLO attempts to undermine support for Israel while pleading its own cause through its representatives at the United Nations. On November 13, 1974, though not a permanent member of the United Nations, the PLO was able to persuade the General Assembly to invite Yasir Arafat to address it. Arafat told the delegates that he came "bearing an olive branch and a freedom fighter's gun." The PLO representatives at the United Nations have also tried to secure censuring resolutions against Israel in U.N. organizations such as United Nations Educational, Scientific and Cultural Organization (UNESCO), and the International Labor Organization (ILO). On November 10, 1975, the PLO succeeded in mobilizing the Arab, Communist, and Third World delegates in the General Assembly for the passage of a resolution declaring that "Zionism is a form of racism and racial discrimination."

How have the Arab governments reacted to the Palestinian Movement's demand for autonomy within the Arab countries?

Since the June 1967 Six-Day War, Jordan and Lebanon have been the principal bases for launching terrorist attacks against Israel. The large concentration of terrorist units in Jordan became intolerable to the government, and in September 1970 the terrorists were expelled after a violent civil war. King Hussein justified this action by stating: "The terrorists behaved not like guests but like masters. . . . Instead of directing their attack against territories occupied by Israel, they waged war against us." Most of these terrorist units relocated in Lebanon, where they found little restraint on their activities.* When their occasional raids on Israel brought retaliatory attacks on their bases in southern Lebanon, the terrorists complained that they were not adequately protected by the Lebanese army.

---

*The 1969 Lebanon and PLO agreement gave the PLO permission for free movement all over Lebanon. It also entitled the PLO to act freely and get assistance from the Lebanese government when they attacked Israel.

This charge contributed to the growing friction between the Moslem population of Lebanon, which supported the terrorists, and the Christian population, which largely favored restraints on terrorist activities. In the civil war that erupted in 1975, the Palestinians fought on the Moslem side.

Did the PLO's 1970 war with King Hussein of Jordan pose a serious threat to Israel's security?

When the PLO appeared on the verge of winning, the threat of a terrorist-controlled Jordan prompted Israel to prepare to move a military force under General Mordecai Gur into Amman, the Jordanian capital, if the guerrillas defeated King Hussein's bedouin army. Alarmed at the possible overthrow of its ally, King Hussein, the U.S. government ordered fifty ships of the Sixth Fleet to stand ready to assist the Israeli forces with materiel. The U.S. Navy flew supplies by helicopter to the Israeli port of Haifa. The threat of this action by the United States and Israel forced the Syrians who had mobilized a tank movement of 250 to 300 tanks* against Jordan to withdraw and the terrorists to flee.

What decision gave the PLO authority in the West Bank?

At the Arab summit conference in Rabat, Morocco on September 29, 1974, King Hussein of Jordan was forced to renounce his claim to the West Bank area which had been part of Jordan from 1948 to 1967, and agreed in the joint Arab statement that the political operations within this territory would be placed under PLO supervision "as the sole legitimate representative of the Palestinian people."

---

*The largest number used in any military operations to that date.

What has been the position of the U.S. government on relations with the PLO?

As policy, the U.S. government does not consider the PLO a legitimate participant in Middle East peace negotiations as long as the PLO refuses to acknowledge Israel's right to exist as a sovereign state.

Has the PLO changed or moderated its position of never accepting an Israeli state?

At its founding in 1964, the PLO declared in Article 21 of the Palestine National Covenant: "The Arab Palestinian people, expressing themselves by the armed Palestinian revolution, rejects all solutions which are substitutes for the total liberation of Palestine. . . ."

In *The New York Times* of February 17, 1976, Saleh Khalef, second-in-command to Yasir Arafat, declared: "There is something the world must know. Let us all die, let us all be killed, let us all be assassinated, but we will not recognize Israel." In its loss of power following Syrian control of Lebanon, the PLO has indicated a desire to modify its inflexible position against Israel.

Does the PLO qualify as a government-in-exile?

In order to be a government-in-exile it would first have to have been a government in actuality; that is a government in residence and operation within a recognized sovereign state. The PLO has never met any of these qualifications, and although its claim to government-in-exile status may be recognized by certain nations, in practical terms, the PLO represents only itself.

Did the civil war in Lebanon affect the PLO terrorist activity against Israel?

In its struggle in Lebanon, the PLO lost its last territorial foothold and its military base against Israel. The massive encampments which the Palestinians constructed in southern Lebanon, ostensibly for launching attacks against the Israeli enemy, have been neutralized if not totally destroyed. The Palestinian base-in-exile has been demolished in Lebanon in the summer of 1976 as thoroughly as it was in Jordan in the "Black September" of 1970.

Does a terrorist organization need a territorial base of its own to ensure continuous and effective operation?

The PLO's experience in Jordan in 1970 and more recently in Lebanon demonstrates that a terrorist organization which must continually depend on the patronage of host countries faces not only serious threats to its freedom of action, but to its very existence. From its inception in 1964, the PLO has been subject to external controls; first by Egypt and then by Jordan, where attempts to limit the PLO's power culminated in the expulsion of the terrorist organization. In 1976 it found itself involved in a protracted civil war in Lebanon, unable to carry out its basic mission—terrorist operations against Israel. When Syria entered the conflict and turned against the PLO and its leftist armies, once again, as in Jordan, PLO guerrillas were forced to fight for their lives against the army of an Arab country (Syria) which had previously been among the PLO's staunchest supporters.

What was the exact nature of PLO involvement in the Lebanese conflict?

The PLO sided with Moslem forces against the Maronite Christian army which appeared at the beginning of the conflict to be the winning side. This raised the possibility of Lebanon's being taken over by the radical left-wing coalition of Moslems and the PLO. However, the military balance was reversed in favor of the rightist Christians when Syria intervened militarily to forestall the possibility of Lebanon's becoming another radical left-wing state on Syria's western border.

What has happened to the PLO as a result of its participation in the Lebanese civil war?

The PLO suffered so serious a defeat at the hands of the Maronite Christians and Syria that its influence in the Middle East has been blunted in the Arab-Israeli conflict. In the agreement at a meeting of six Arab leaders in Riyadh late in October 1976, Syria was permitted to maintain military control of Lebanon. The PLO found itself "homeless" under control of Syria. It dreams of the notorious "Protocols" calling for dismemberment of Israel and the establishment of a secular state have been called into question by "moderate" Arab nations.

What effect did the PLO have on the Arab political conflict in Lebanon?

The PLO has proved to be a destructive element in the entire fabric of the Arab world. According to Premier Yitzhak Rabin of Israel, "Lebanon was the only secular country in the Arab world in which Christians and Moslems could live together and the PLO has destroyed that coexistence."

What has happened to Arafat's concept of a Palestine state?

Arafat's dream of creating a secular state to include Jordan and Israel as well as Palestine has become a nightmare. Even his toned-down effort to accommodate his proposed Palestine state to Israel as a neighbor is seen with a jaundiced eye by moderate Arab leaders as well as Israel. This "softening" by PLO of its opposition to Israel's existence is regarded by Israelis as merely tactical. According to Professor Yehoshafat Harkabi, an Israeli expert on the Palestinians and a government adviser, 15 of the 33 articles in the PLO convenant still call for the destruction of Israel either explicitly or implicitly.

Will the PLO still be able to assert itself and disrupt the efforts of the United States and the moderate Arab states toward a peaceful settlement in the area?

The PLO can still be a fly in the Middle East ointment. With its footloose anarchy, Arafat's threat to go underground and resort to overground methods (terrorism), his ability to explode efforts to establish a Palestinian state which the PLO does not dominate may disrupt peacemaking efforts of the United States and moderate Arab leaders.

7

Soviet Gains and Setbacks in the Middle East

What country has caused the greatest mischief in recent Middle East history?

The Soviet Union.

How?

By supplying her Arab clients with massive modern military arsenals running into billions of dollars to generate and make war against Israel.

Could the Arab nations have mounted these assaults without the Soviet war materiel?

No Arab government was prepared to cope with the sophisticated military machine and the high-geared training of the Israelis. The most powerful, Egypt, its 38,000,000 population in dire and increasing poverty, had no source other than the Soviets to secure modern weaponry or the training for its use supplied by the Russian officers.

Why did the Russians provide and resupply this prodigious arsenal to the Arab nations?

Russia's goal to become the dominant power in the Middle East called for a strategy of rivalry and upheaval in the area. As a newcomer and a democracy, Israel provided the perfect target for increasing hostility from Arabs.

Does the Kremlin seek the destruction and elimination of Israel?

No. Without a target for her Arab clients to shoot at, her strategy of keeping the area in tumult so as to keep her hand at the throttle and dominate the moves in the area could not succeed.

What has been at the core of Kremlin aspiration in the Middle East for two centuries?

A warm-water outlet has been an age-old obsession of the Russians since Catherine the Great and the succeeding czars. The Communist leaders embraced this heritage as an article of faith.

What unexpected door opened for the Russians to begin to get a foothold in the region?

Its affirmative vote on November 29, 1947 at the U.N. General Assembly for partition of the disputed area between Arabs and Jews in Palestine.

Did the United States vote yes at the same time?

Only after its effort to renege from its original agreement to support Israel statehood. Moscow's unremitting pressure to assist in the creation of the State of Israel against U.S. and Arab opposition was the principal instrument bringing the new nation into being.

In the light of her historic tradition of anti-Semitism, why did Moscow take this strong position in favor of the creation of a Jewish state?

Moscow saw the birth of Israel as a means of dislodging the British from the Middle East. She hoped also to lure the new state into her political orbit by virtue of Israel's socialist tendencies in her *kibbutzim* (collective farms).

Did the Soviet ploy succeed?

No. The democratic government of Israel, patterned after Great Britain and the United States, chose to ally itself with the Western democracies, principally the United States, which became her great benefactor.

What was Moscow's first confrontation with the United States in the Middle East?

President Nasser's violent opposition to the Baghdad Pact,* a British inspired anti-Soviet alliance backed by the United States that omitted Egypt, took the form of a $250,000,000 arms agreement with the U.S.S.R. It succeeded eventually in outflanking the Baghdad Pact.

How did the Russians gain access to the region?

President Nasser accepted the Russians' offer to finance and build the giant Aswan Dam in 1958. This fol-

---

*In a meeting with President Nasser in his home outside of Cairo in 1955 he fulminated against the pact and swore that he would dispose of Nuri el Said, its leader. In 1958 Nuri was assassinated and his body dragged through the streets of Baghdad.

lowed long negotiations between Secretary of State John Foster Dulles, who abruptly terminated them. Nasser's reaction was to open the door to the Soviets and to seize the Suez Canal.

How did Moscow outmaneuver the U.S. in the Suez crisis?

In 1956, after Nasser's seizure of the Canal, Britain, France and Israel engaged in a three-pronged attack to repossess it. Russian threatened to blow up the area if the attackers did not retreat. President Eisenhower and Secretary Dulles, who had never been consulted by our allies before the assault, decided not to call Moscow's bluff and forced the British and French and Israelis to retreat.

How did Nasser fare in this maneuver?

The combined pressure from Moscow and Washington transformed his defeat into a personal triumph. He had lost the war—in fact, resigned as president—but the Moscow-Washington intervention was a lifeline that put him back in power.

How did Moscow help generate the 1967 Six-Day War?

Principally, by supplying Egypt with a $12 billion modern arsenal along with technicians to train her armies and airmen in the use of the modern weaponry and aircraft.

What did Moscow do after the Egyptian defeat?

She decided at once to replenish and rebuild the Egyptian military arsenal for another assault on Israel.

What was the Soviet-Egyptian friendship treaty of May 27, 1971? Did it remain intact?

This fifteen-year treaty provided for uninterrupted military aid to Egypt. But on July 8, 1972, President Sadat abrogated the treaty and ordered the Russians out of Egypt, accusing them of reneging on promises for essential armament support.

How did the Soviets and the United States confront each other in the 1973 Yom Kippur War?

When the Israeli army unexpectedly crossed the Suez and beleaguered the Egyptian Third Army, the Russians threatened to intervene unless the United States would succeed in pressing the Israelis to break the siege.

How did the United States react to the Russian threat?

Secretary of State Kissinger forced the Israelis to withdraw after they had surrounded the Egyptian Third Army, thus handing the Egyptians an unearned victory.

What did Moscow achieve from its enormous investment in Egypt?

The right to use the Suez Canal (opened to every country expect Israel) for Soviet ships to move down the Persian Gulf oil territory and the Indian Ocean. She also managed to inflict a wound on Israel's manpower, position, economy, and prestige.

What is the Kremlin strategy in driving to the Persian Gulf?

By gaining control of the oil lifelines on which the European nations (and the United States) depend for their economic subsistence, she can paralyze these democratic nations and force them into her orbit.

Is the Kremlin in need of oil?

Not today. As the world's second largest producer and an exporter of oil, she has an oversupply. But according to some Soviet and Eastern European experts, the Russian demand for oil will exceed her supply in 1980 by 100,000,000 barrels a day.

How did the United States capitalize on the ouster of the Russians from Egypt?

In the disarmament pact worked out by Secretary of State Kissinger with the Egyptians and Israelis on September 1, 1975, the United States replaced the Russians as Egypt's ally, providing President Sadat with major financing and support. As part of the disengagement agreement, the United States was permitted to station 200 American technicians in the zone of separation in the Sinai, thus injecting a U.S. foothold in the region for the first time.

Have the Russians advanced their naval strength in the Mediterranean?

The Bear has learned to swim. Since 1960 the Russian Navy has been modernized and moved in strength into the warm-water ports as a full-fledged competitor of the U.S. Sixth Fleet. The Kremlin has continued a concerted buildup of its navy to cope with and outdistance the U.S. Sixth Fleet in the Mediterranean.

What recent major addition to its squadron will significantly strengthen it?

Its first aircraft carrier, the 40,000-ton *Kiev*. The YAK-36 fighters aboard are designed for short take-off and landing (STOLs).

Has the *Kiev* affected the naval balance in the Mediterranean?*

It is only the first of four carriers the Soviets will launch as a challenge to the United States, which has enjoyed an advantage in the Mediterranean with its carriers, the U.S.S. *Nimitz,* the U.S.S. *America,* the U.S.S. *Forrestal,* the U.S.S. *Independence,* the U.S.S. *John F. Kennedy,* the U.S.S. *Franklin D. Roosevelt,* and the U.S.S. *Saratoga,* two of which alternate in the Mediterranean every six months.

What can Russia now do with its big new navy as part of its strategy to close a pincers around the Middle East?

It has jumped into the future by building large numbers of nuclear powered submarines. Russia's navy also enables it to attempt a selective blockade in the Middle East like the United States mounted against her in the Cuba crisis of 1962.

Is the United States aware of the meaning of this effort at encirclement of the Sixth Fleet by the Soviet navy's expansion?

The US. Navy officials are. But they have not been able to "educate" the American public who still see the

---

*In 1974, Admiral Zumwalt, former Chief of Naval Operations, sent this writer on a private mission with the Sixth Fleet in the Mediterranean to inspect and submit a report to him on the Soviet ships tailing the U.S. ships.

Mediterranean as an American "lake" controlled by the Sixth Fleet's aircraft carriers and destroyers. According to Elmo R. Zumwalt, the retired Navy Chief of Operations, if the U.S. Navy had battled the Soviet Navy in the Mediterranean during the Yom Kippur War of 1973, "the odds are very high that they would have won and we would have lost."

What is the numerical strength between the two navies' surface ships?

The present strength of the Soviet squadron, which is drawn from the Black Sea Fleet, is 56 surface ships and an undisclosed number of submarines. The present strength of the U.S. Sixth Fleet is 43 ships plus submarines.

Why has the Kremlin provided undeviating support to the PLO?

As part of the Russian strategic calculations to gain a base in the heart of the Middle East, it has used the PLO as a surrogate and provides it with vast supplies of arms.

What was behind the Soviet Union's support of the PLO in the Lebanese crisis?

The Kremlin's goals were politically tied to the PLO and her left-wing Moslem allies. Against the Moslems and their Soviet backing, the Christian Maronites had the support from the moderate Arab nations: Saudi Arabia, Kuwait, Jordan, Egypt, and Syria. The United States, which had consistently supported the established Lebanese regime, came to her aid through the undisclosed assistance of Israel, which was called upon to supply the Maronites with military equipment via the Mediterranean.

How has the Russian strategy operated with the African Third World?

Russia has corralled the majority of the upcoming African nations to her side as evidenced in their overwhelming votes in her favor of the United Nations. The Kremlin acts as a supplier of armaments for these nations—including Uganda, the scene of the spectacular Entebbe rescue. Somalia, an island strategically located in the heart of Africa, is a Soviet ally, where the Russians have a missile repair facility.

How has the Kremlin's position with the Arabs deteriorated since its estrangement from Cairo?

Russia turned to Syria, which accepted her assistance in munitions but refused to tie herself to the Russian Bear. But the Kremlin's influence with Syria eroded when President Assad asserted his own independence by intervening unilaterally in Lebanon. (Moscow maintains a continuous close tie with her other Arab clients: Iraq, Libya, and the PLO.) Moscow was reduced to a spectator's role as she was forced to watch two of her "clients"—the Syrians, who pulled away from her; and the Palestinians, whom she backed politically and materially—fight each other with Soviet weapons.

Why did Moscow urge the reconvening of a Geneva peacemaking conference?

She was to share a joint chairmanship with the United States, placing her in an equal position to swing her influence for her Arab clients and the PLO against the United States and Israel.

How was the Geneva meeting sidetracked?

The Israelis' refusal to attend was supported by the U.S. as long as the PLO covenant called for the "elimination of Israel."

Is it war or peace that the Soviet Union seeks in the Middle East?

Either would be a severe brake on her goal of strategic domination of the area. Keeping the region in turmoil through agitating and supporting her Arab clients to assault Israel provides Moscow with the leverage to call strategic signals in the area. If there is peace in the Middle East, there is no room for the Soviet Union.

Have the Russians lost any manpower in their manifold operations in the area?

Not a single man that can be accounted for. Her strategy of supplying the guns for "the other fellow" to do the fighting and dying has been eminently successful.

How did the Russians manage to manipulate the Arabs into keeping the area in tumult?

The Kremlin capitalized on the rivalry between the Arabs, playing one against the other and their common enemy, Israel. When she was evicted from Egypt, Moscow turned to Syria and then to Libya, Sadat's enemy on her border, and supplied their leader Qaddafi with major arms. Moscow's game had a temporary setback as the internecine fighting of Arab against Arab distracted them from their number-one target, Israel, the only objective upon which all Arabs have been able to agree.

What has been Moscow's purpose in collaborating with Libya?

To help Libya challenge Egypt on their border. Qaddafi, Libya's volatile leader who has publicly sworn that Communism is his number-one enemy, was supplied with major arms by the Kremlin in a deal unmatched for cynicism even in the Middle East. Ironically, both Egyptian and Libyan forces face each other on their border with Soviet-made arms.

What effect did the Soviet Union's entrance into the Middle East have on Israel?

Without Moscow's immense armament supply, the Arabs, with their paucity of weapons and technical skills, would have been unable to launch their virulent attacks on Israel. As long as the Kremlin continues to play its game with the Arabs against Israel, the chances for peace in the Middle East are diminished.

To what extent has the U.S.S.R. suffered from the defeat of the Arabs in the wars against Israel?

Soviet strategy to use the Arabs as spearheads in their "divide and conquer" program to control the region has been side-tracked.

Have these setbacks in Soviet strategy served to divert her from her aspirations in the Middle East?

With the Kremlin's drive deflected by hostilities in Lebanon, she lost a principal instrument of her bargaining power with her Arab clients. In the light of her cardinal policy to move unrelentingly to the warm water Mediterranean ports, Soviet reverses from her collaboration with the Arabs can only be temporary.

Since the civil war in Lebanon, have the Soviet Union's alliances with her Arab clients changed?

Russia's estrangement from Egypt, the linchpin of Kremlin strategy in the region, has been followed by deteriorating relations with Syria who ousted the Soviet-armed PLO in her fight against the Maronite Christians in Lebanon. Iraq, once a staunch ally, has edged away from the Soviets, leaving Moscow with Libya, a virulent enemy of Communism, as the Kremlin's best "friend."

How is the U.S. competing with the Soviet in the Middle East?

U.S. policy aims to outbid Moscow in bribing Arabs for friendship. To cope with Soviet momentum in the region, U.S. efforts may be "too little and too late."

What was the painful lesson Russia learned from her imperial Middle East venture?

"You can't buy an Arab, you can only rent him." (Quote from a State Department report written by the author following a survey in the Middle East.)

8

Inter-Arab Rivalry

What is the main obstacle to peace in the Middle East?

It is not Israel. It is the national ambitions and the traditional hatred and rivalries which dominate the Arab world.

What forms do inter-Arab rivalries take?

Territorial disputes between neighboring Arab countries, political and dynastic feuds, rivalries for leadership of the Arab world, civil wars provoked or exploited by other Arab countries.

How did the rivalry between today's Arab states begin?

The Arab countries of the Middle East came into being as modern states after the breakup of the Ottoman empire at the end of World War I. However, from 1918 to almost the beginning of World War II, these states were under British and French mandates, and as such were pawns in the power struggle between the two European nations. The practice of the British and French was to set the various Arab princes or leaders against each other, aggravating or capitalizing on existing Arab feuds or creating new ones. Once set in motion, these Arab rivalries continued after the mandate territories received their independence, beginning with Iraq in 1930 and culminating with Transjordan in 1946.

What are some of the rivalries that were fomented in the period between the world wars?

The Syrians believe that Lebanon was an integral part of Syria, but had been set up as a separate country by the French to provide autonomy for the dominant Christian population at the expense of the Moslems. The Syrians also consider Jordan and Palestine as being historically part of south Syria.

The rulers of Iraq dreamed of dominating a region composed of Syria, Lebanon, and Jordan as part of their own country.

The dynasty that rules Saudi Arabia today won the vast Arabian peninsula from the Hashemite dynasty in 1924, creating a lasting enmity between the two families. King Hussein of Jordan is the grandson of the expelled Hashemite ruler. Another Hashemite king ruled Iraq before being overthrown in the 1950s, and his enemies included the Saudi king, the Syrian leaders, and the Egyptians, who have traditionally vied with the Iraqis for leadership of the Arab world.

Were these rivalries suspended during World War II?

No. In 1942 Nuri el Said of Iraq proposed a union of the countries of the Fertile Crescent (Lebanon, Syria, Iraq) which was opposed by both Egypt and Saudi Arabia. Egypt feared the Iraqis would dominate this union and increase Iraqi influence in the Arab world at the expense of her own. The Saudis reacted against the scheme because it would benefit its Hashemite rival, Iraq.

In 1944 Egypt proposed the formation of an organization to coordinate the policies of the Arab states toward the outside world, and the following year the Arab League was founded composed of Egypt, Syria, Lebanon, Iraq, Jordan, Saudi Arabia, and Yemen. The League has been ineffectual, and its affairs have been dominated by the Egyptian-Iraqi power struggle and the Saudi-Hashemite dynastic feud. Recent additions to the League include Libya, Algeria, Tunisia, Morocco, Sudan, and Somalia.

How did this rivalry develop in the post–World War II period?

The needs of the Americans and British to secure a Middle East base against Soviet expansion led to the proposal of an alliance of the states of the Middle East's "northern tier": Iraq, Turkey and Pakistan. Known as the Baghdad Pact,* it inflamed the Egyptian-Iraqi rivalry by threatening Egypt's leadership in the Arab League. Egypt's President Nasser tried to set up his own area defense organization with Syria and Saudi Arabia as an Arab counterpart of the Baghdad Pact, and although this attempt had little real consequence, it did demonstrate Nasser's potential for popular leadership in the Arab world.

Was Nasser able to overcome the traditional rivalry of the Arab world?

In 1958 the Baathist leaders of Syria pressured Nasser into merging Egypt and Syria resulting in a political coalition called the United Arab Republic (U.A.R.). The Baathists were looking for a leader with sufficient stature to win the support of the Syrian public and save the country from the growing Communist influ-

---

*At my meeting with the late President Nasser in his home in 1955, his fulminations against the United States centered around our support of the Baghdad Pact which omitted Egypt. He indicated that he would find the way to dispose of the pact's leader Nuri el Said, who was assassinated in 1958.

ence, and they were convinced that Nasser was their only hope. However, inherent rivalries between the ruling factions of both countries could not be suppressed, and the union came apart two years later. In a revolution in Iraq the king and Nasser's bitter rival Nuri el Said were assassinated, and the Baathist regime that succeeded appeared to be taking its example from Nasser; but Iraqi nationalism quickly became anti-Nasser, and the traditional rivalry between Iraq and Egypt was restored.

When did Lebanon first become a battleground of Arab rivalries?

In 1958 tensions between the Christian and Moslem factions of Lebanon broke out into armed conflict. The Moslem groups looked to President Nasser of Egypt for support, and the Christian-controlled government looked to the United States for help. The Egyptians and Syrians exploited the situation in Lebanon to further the influence of the revolutionary regimes such as their own and the Iraqi Baathists who had just come into power, over the Western-leaning governments of Lebanon and Jordan. The United States sent troops to Lebanon and the British dispatched troops to Jordan, with orders to do nothing but protect the governments of the two countries. The crisis in Lebanon quickly subsided, and the U.S. and British troops were withdrawn.

Do the Arabs curtail their rivalry when dealing with their enemy Israel?

In the first encounter with Israel in 1948, the armies of the neighboring Arab countries that invaded the new Jewish state did so not primarily to protect the Palestinians but to prevent each other from expanding their territories. After the Sinai agreements between Egypt and Israel in 1975, Syria and Iraq characterized the result as a betrayal of the Arab cause as each sought to wrest the leadership of the Arab world from Egypt. The one thing the Arabs agree on is opposition to Israel; but they disagree on the exact means to destroy her. States such as Egypt and Saudi Arabia hope the United States will reduce Israel to a manageable foe, while the more impatient leaders of Iraq and Libya, safely removed from Israel's reach, deride the diplomatic tactics and advocate an aggressive military solution.

Does the Palestine issue unite the Arab states in spite of their inherent rivalries?

Rather than unite them, the Palestine issue tends to aggravate their rivalry. Each claims to be the true champion of the Palestinian cause and accuses its current rival of insufficient dedication or outright betrayal. Also, the fear exists that one Arab government might provoke hostilities with Israel that might unintentionally drag another government into a conflict.

Do the Arabs cooperate with each other in scheming against Israel?

The Arabs scheme against each other more effectively than against Israel. As an example, at the Arab summit conference in Rabat, Morocco, in October 1974, the Arab leaders, fearing that Hussein and Israel might come to an agreement on the West Bank and Gaza territories without the sanction of other Arab countries, decided to name the PLO as "sole negotiator" for the Palestinian people in the region. King Hussein left the meeting convinced that this decision "would lead them up a blind alley" in dealing with Israel. The king's political sagacity again proved to be more realistic than that of all the Arab leaders.

Has Saudi Arabia played any part in reconciling Arab rivalries?

The Saudis succeeded at the Riyadh Conference in late October 1976 in patching up the rift between Egypt and Syria, thus reconstructing the united front against Israel. The Saudis used their enormous oil wealth to pay off the Egyptians and the Syrians to build a new alliance and dampen these inter-Arab rivalries. The Saudis' greatest concern is the danger of Communist intrusion into the Arab world and the Soviet's exploitation of Arab quarrels.

What are the rivalries between the Arab countries of North Africa?

The rivalry between Algeria and Morocco has been inflamed by the takeover of the Spanish-held western Sahara by Morocco (and Mauritania) after an agreement reached with Spain. The Algerians have reacted by stirring up desert tribes and arming them for raids on Moroccan outposts. This violent reaction occurs because Algeria regards itself as the dominant power in North Africa and resents Moroccan expansion, particularly when the territory includes one of the richest deposits of phosphates in the world. Morocco and Tunisia, which flank Algeria on the west and east, are blocking Algeria's vital economic projects to supply natural gas to Spain and Italy through pipelines that would run across these neighboring Arab countries.

Which Arab leader provokes the greatest hostility among the other Arab states?

Colonel Muammar el-Qaddafi of Libya has earned the enmity of most of the other Arab leaders by plotting against the governments of Egypt,* Jordan, Saudi Arabia, and Morocco; by sponsoring an abortive coup in Sudan in which hundreds of people were killed, and by contributing to the carnage in Lebanon by providing the Moslems with immense amounts of money and guns. He has sent his agents to attempt assassination of the leaders of Tunisia and Egypt. President Sadat and other Arab leaders have publicly called Colonel Qaddafi a lunatic, and speak of assisting anti-Qaddafi Libyans in a coup to overthrow him.

Do the Arabs prefer to fight each other rather than Israel?

Four wars with Israel consumed less time than the Arabs have devoted to fighting each other in Lebanon alone. The Palestinians, who claim to be at war with Israel to regain their homeland, have shown that they prefer to fight the armies of Jordan and Lebanon rather than the army of Israel. King Hussein of Jordan, justifying the expulsion of the Palestinians in 1970, stated: "Instead of directing their attacks against the territories occupied by Israel, they [the Palestinians] waged war against us; you'd have thought they'd mistaken Jordan for Israel, that they were practicing resistance here where they were safe."†

Do Arab rivalries cost many Arab lives?

The Palestinians' attempt to take over Jordan from King Hussein in September 1970 and the ensuing massacre resulted in the loss of 3,600 lives in just a

---

*In August 1976 Arab gunmen hijacked an Egyptian airliner and ordered the pilot to fly it to Libya. After Egyptian paratroops thwarted the attempt and released 80 hostage passengers, authorities reported the captured hijackers as saying they had acted on orders of Colonel Qaddafi, who had promised them $250,000 if they forced the plane to land at Benghazi.

†From an interview by Oriana Fallaci, *N.Y. Post,* January 18, 1975.

few weeks; more Arabs killed by Arabs than had died in the 1967 Six-Day War with Israel.* In Lebanon, over 50,000 Arabs were killed in the civil war which began in 1975.

What are some other examples of conflict within the Arab world?

The Kurds of Iraq, a non-Arab minority numbering in the millions, are fighting the Iraqis for an autonomous state of their own. Border clashes and civil wars flare up intermittently in the Persian Gulf sheikdoms. About 500,000 deaths resulted from a civil war in Sudan that went on for 17 years. In Yemen, Arabs slaughtered each other with Egypt's help a few years ago. Somalia, too, is fighting with its African neighbors.

Which Arab border most personifies inter-Arab rivalry?

The border between Syria and Iraq has been the scene of a long and bitter rivalry involving territorial disputes and controversies over water rights. The present regimes of both countries are rival factions of the Baathist party, and each purports to be the only true advocate of that party's political ideology. Each country stations large military contingents at their mutual border, thus creating constant tension. The Syrian involvement in Lebanon is due in great part to this hostility; a leftist-Palestinian takeover there would leave Syria sandwiched between Iraq and a pro-Iraqi regime in Lebanon.

---

*Nasser had to remind his fellow Arabs that they should be killing Jews in Haifa and Tel Aviv, not each other in the streets of Amman.

What latent rivalries has Syria's intervention in Lebanon aroused?

Egypt's pretensions to leadership of the Arab world would be diminished by Syrian success in its Lebanese venture. Also a feared revival of Syrian ambitions for a "Greater Syria" embracing Lebanon, and possibly Iraq, Jordan, and a reconquered Palestine, first advocated in the 1940s, is suspected as Syria's ultimate intention.

What were the major elements of Arab rivalry in the Lebanese civil war?

The war in Lebanon was a microcosm of the pattern of rivalries that wrack the Arab world. It was the showdown for the arrogant, freewheeling PLO which tried to take over Jordan and, failing that, threw in its lot with a Moslem faction in an effort to bring down the Lebanese government. The struggle between the Palestinians and the traditional Arab governments that have offered them sanctuary reached its climax in Lebanon in the upheaval in 1975. While other Arab governments were critical of Jordan for killing Palestinians in 1970 when the king evicted the PLO, they were silent in the Lebanese civil war. Egypt now accuses Syria as a betrayer of the Palestinians' cause just as Syria had done against Egypt after the Sinai agreements with Israel. Old enemies Syria and Iraq allied themselves with opposing Lebanese factions. But the salient fact is that the Civil War never really ended; the conflict between the Moslem and Christian Arabs is irreconcilable; the embers can burst into flame at any time.

Why did Arabs kill Arabs with such hatred in the Lebanese war?

Beneath the facade of coexistence in Lebanon there existed a pent-up hatred and resentment between the Moslem and Christian Arab populations. The Moslem Arab, who considers himself a true Arab, looks upon the Christian Arab as an alien. The Moslems resented a government that permitted an alien segment of the Arab population—the Christians—to control it and the wealth of their country.

What did the Moslem Arabs do to attempt to take control?

They were unable to act until the influx of the Palestinian refugees—who are Moslems—gave them a majority over the Christians. All the years of frustration and animosity erupted into fighting, which quickly became a carnage unparalleled in the history of civil warfare. The 50,000 dead exceeded the total Arab loss in the four wars against Israel.

What were the economic factors in this Moslem-Christian rivalry in Lebanon?

The immense financial gains that the controlling Maronite leaders enjoyed from the increasing oil proceeds had long been a target of the left-wing Moslems. The Lebanese in power have regularly received a percentage from every gallon of the oil flowing through the pipelines in Tripoli in the north of the country.

Since the flow of billions to the oil moguls, what new rivalry is emerging in the Arab world?

The millions of "have-not" Arabs had every reason to expect to share in some measure from the prodigious volume of oil money pouring into the coffers of the "haves." The Arab shieks' denial to the masses of any of the fruits of the new wealth has stirred up an undercurrent of unrest abetted by Communist infiltration that presages a new element in Arab rivalries from within the oil-rich nations.

9

Israel as Neighbor and Ally

What is Israel's value as a Middle East nation?

As a useful and needed neighbor, she has demonstrated that she can be more valuable to the Arab nations as a friend than as an enemy.

Is Israel a bona fide member of the Middle East community of nations?

Historically and demographically, Israel is a Middle East nation. As of the last census, Israel's population is composed nearly 50 percent of native-born (Sabra). Of the rest, 23.2 percent were born in Asia and Africa, and 27.5 percent in Europe and America. The number of Sabras has undoubtedly increased since this last census was taken in 1972.

What is Israel's current position in the Middle East community?

Israel is a democracy under siege. The Arab countries and terrorist organizations which seek to destroy Israel represent various forms of nondemocratic autocracies and military dictatorships. For Daniel P.

Moynihan, former U.S. ambassador to the United Nations and now senator from New York, "The point is that Israel has become a metaphor for democracy. The determination of the totalitarians and the despotisms to destroy Israel is directed at all of us."*

As a democracy, how does Israel defend itself?

Israel's army is solely for defense. It maintains a small standing army and relies upon a civilian reserve army, such as the Minutemen were in the American Revolutionary War, which it quickly mobilizes only when threatened by attack.

What was the genesis of today's Israeli army?

The modern Israeli army grew out of the Haganah (Defense) which was developed in the 1920s to defend the Jewish settlements from Arab attack.

How does Israel open its doors to Arab society today?

Israel's policy toward Arabs is best expressed by Chaim Herzog, its ambassador to the United Nations: "I can point with pride to the Arab ministers who have served in my government, to Arab officers and men serving of their own volition in our defense border and police forces, frequently commanding Jewish troops, to the hundreds of thousands of Arabs from all over the Middle East crowding the cities of Israel every year, to the thousands of Arabs from all over the Middle East coming for medical treatment to the Hadassah Hospital in Jerusalem and other hospitals. To the peaceful coexistence which has developed. To the fact that

---

*New York Magazine, July 26, 1976.

Arabic is an official language in Israel on a par with Hebrew."*

How did doctors from Hadassah Hospital administer to Lebanese victims in the "Open Fences" policy of Israel?

Israel set up clinics at the borders of Metulla, Israel's northernmost town adjacent to Lebanon, and Har Dovev where doctors from Hadassah Hospital treated more than 5,000 Lebanese (both Christians and Moslems) without payment during the Lebanese civil war.

How is Israel showing itself to be a useful member of the Middle East community?

In spite of living under siege since the day of its birth, twenty-eight years ago, Israel has sought to demonstrate its intentions to be a good neighbor. Since June 1967 Israel has maintained an "Open Bridges" policy which allows the movement of people and goods between the West Bank and Jordan. Currently, over 100,000 Jordanians a year make this crossing. Open bridges over the Jordan River permit regular trade with the Arab countries and free movement of persons either way, for family reunion, work, or study.

What is a more recent example?

The Lebanese victims of the civil war who flocked to the borders of Israel found "open fences." Israel freely offered hospitals, food and refuge to her wounded and sick Lebanese neighbors. The two former belligerents also began to conduct commercial business between

---

*Speech by Ambassador Chaim Herzog to the General Assembly November 10, 1975.

them when Israel removed the barriers. With Lebanon's industry ravaged by civil war, its reconstruction can be expedited and modernized by the acceptance of Israel's offer of assistance.

How did Israel come to the aid of the Lebanese government under siege in the civil war?

Despite the fact that Lebanon is not at peace with Israel, at the request of the U.S. government, Israel supplied essential critical military equipment, most of which it shipped via the Mediterranean. Israel saw the PLO, which was on the verge of taking over Lebanon, as a major potential threat on its northern border.

What other examples of potential valuable interchange can be cited?

The medical formula developed in Israel to prevent blindness from trachoma, a disease which afflicts every fourth child in Egypt, was offered to President Nasser by the writer in one of his visits. It was specified that the fact that it came from Israel would be kept secret. Nevertheless, it was rejected as being unacceptable because it came from an "enemy country." The rejection condemned future generations of thousands of Egyptians to inevitable blindness.

How could Egypt—its largest neighbor—benefit from peace with Israel?

As long as Egypt maintains its belligerency toward Israel, it cannot take advantage of the Arab markets lying to the east of Israel, which would vastly improve the impoverished Egyptian economy.

How could Jordan's economy prosper from Israel as a good neighbor?

Jordan, which does not have its own seaport, would have the port of Haifa's facilities from which to develop overseas commerce. Even in a state of belligerency, there is an extensive exchange of goods and services which has benefited both people's economy. In a state of peace, this beginning of commerce across the Jordan River would be greately increased to the mutual advantage of both countries.

How would completely open borders between Israel and her Arab neighbors benefit everyone?

People who visit Israel now are not allowed to visit Arab countries. Even diplomatic personnel must detour through Cyprus to cross from Israel to an Arab state. Peace in the Middle East would open these borders, allowing tourists and businessmen to travel freely throughout the area. The economic benefits to each country in the area would be incalculable.

What value can the scientific developments in Israel have for the Middle Eastern community?

They can serve to help improve the quality of life for the people in the region. As a peaceful neighbor, Israel would share the fruits of its broad advances in the technological field and would allow an exchange of information between Arab and Israeli scientists.

How can Israel help solve the problem of the vast useless Arab deserts?

Israel has developed new techniques of desalinating water to pump into the desert which can be adapted to the urgent needs of the Arabs to cultivate vast deserts for essential food.

As a good neighbor, what benefit could Israel offer to the Arab youth?

Its many sophisticated universities and technical institutes would be open to all Arab students. With a population of 3,000,000 (including 850,000 Arabs), there are 8 universities and technical institutes in Israel. The educational facilities from these schools can be made available to neighbor Arabs along with the benefits from the faculty experience, interchange, etc.

How does Israel help serve the best interests of the United States in the Middle East?

Israel has shown itself to be a consistent and dependable U.S. ally in the Middle East in contrast to the Arab countries, most of whom have demonstrated their vulnerability to the manipulations of the Soviet Union.

How does Israel aid the U.S. strategic position in the Middle East?

"Whoever controls the Mediterranean, controls the Middle East."* The U.S. Sixth Fleet in the Mediterranean is the only U.S. presence in the Middle East.

---

*Stated to me by Admiral Zumwalt in my meeting with him at the Pentagon prior to my mission on the Sixth Fleet.

It guards our political and economic interests in the region. In contrast to the Russian fleet in the Mediterranean, which enjoys a number of friendly ports, there is only one port facility that is guaranteed to the Sixth Fleet; the port of Haifa in Israel.

How could Israel as an ally help protect vital U.S.. economic interests in the Middle East?

Should the Russians' strategy to cut off the Persian Gulf oil sources to the United States and the Western democracies succeed, the United States may be forced to take drastic military action. In any such event, as an American ally, Israel would provide port facilities for the Sixth Fleet, and its own fully equipped army would be within immediate striking distance.

Has this U.S.-Israeli alliance ever been put into action?

In 1970, when Jordan was in danger of falling into the hands of the Soviet-backed PLO, it was to the mutual interest of the United States and Israel to prevent King Hussein's overthrow. The Israeli armies massed at the Jordanian border to block the PLO from capture of King Hussein's kingdom and the Palestine area. The United States supported the Israeli action with materiel flown into the port of Haifa from Sixth Fleet carriers.

How important are the United States and Israel to each other?

The U.S. is the back bone of Israel at present. The Arabs will not negotiate with a weak Israel. Only a strong, secure Israel can contribute to meaningful negotiations. Without Israel, the United States would lose its only reliable democratic friend in an increasingly pivotal strategic global area for the United States where the Soviets are continuing their drive to gain control of the Persian Gulf.

What major developments in the Middle East are affecting both Israel and the United States as allies?

As the United States resumes its leading role in peacemaking efforts in the area, Israel's position as an ally should be fortified. With strife in Lebanon mainly subsided, the Arabs have shifted their target back to demanding further concessions from Israel on a concerted diplomatic front at Geneva and elsewhere. The two democracies should gain from their mutual aspirations toward recognition of Israel's inalienable right to coexistence.

Appendix

Note 1. In 1949 President Truman proposed a Point Four Program calling for aid to the free peoples of the world to enable them to raise their living standards, and in May 1950 Congress provided $35,000,000 to support his project.

Note 2. In 1953 President Eisenhower appointed Eric Johnston "to undertake discussions with certain of the Arab states and Israel, looking to the mutual development of the water resources of the Jordan River Valley *on a regional basis* for the benefit of all the people of the area." The United States offered to provide up to $200,000,000 toward the plan. It called for about 60 percent of the water to be available to the three Arab states (Syria, Lebanon and Jordan), with 40 percent assigned to Israel. Lebanon and Syria were to receive the full amounts specified by the Arab nations in their 1954 plan to irrigate farms in the headwater region which is the source of the Jordan River. It gave the water Jordan required for the irrigation of all its irrigable land in the Jordan Valley. Israel was allotted unconditional use of what would remain of the Jordan River.

Harnessing the Jordan River as a source of water for Palestine and Trans-Jordan in 1944 was suggested by Dr. Walter Clay Lowdermilk, an American conservationist who had been involved in the United States TVA project. He believed that "large, unused water sources" were available to supply irrigation and power needs in both Palestine and Trans-Jordan.*

Lowdermilk proposed the establishment of a Jordan Valley Authority that

> would divert the sweet waters of the Upper Jordan and its tributaries into a network of irrigation canals, while it would introduce seawater from the Mediterranean . . . for the development of hydroelectric power. . . . Like the TVA, the JVA would be concerned with even more than

---

*Walter Clay Lowdermilk, *Palestine—Land of Promise* (New York and London: Harper & Brothers, 1944).

121

power and irrigation. Its scope would include water conservation; soil conservation through control of erosion; flood control; reforestation; scientific range management and grazing; complete draining of the Huleh swamps; the reclamation of the southern half of Palestine, the Negev, through the damming of flood waters.

The plan never materialized.

Note 3. The declaration was first made known in a letter from British Foreign Secretary Lord Arthur James Balfour to British Zionist leader, Lord Rothschild:

His Majesty's government view with favor the establishment in Palestine of a national home for the Jewish people, and will use their best endeavors to facilitate the achievement of this object, it being clearly understood that nothing shall be done which may prejudice the civil and religious rights and political status enjoyed by Jews in any other country.

Note 4. The Jordanian daily *Filastin* (the Arab name for Palestine), stated on February 19, 1949: "The Arab states, which had encouraged the Palestinian Arabs to leave their homes temporarily in order to be out of the way of the Arab invasion armies ... failed to keep their promises to help these refugees." An extract from a memorandum of the Arab Higher Committee for Palestine on "The Problem of the Arab Refugees" (Cairo, 1952) reads: "Some of the Arab leaders ... declared that they welcomed the immigration of Palestine Arabs into the Arab countries until they saved Palestine. Many of the Palestinian Arabs were misled by these declarations. ..."

Note 5. In his two books, "How Many Refugees?" (London, 1959) and "The Legend of the Arab Refugees" (Tel Aviv, 1967) Dr. Walter Pinner exposed the fraud with these figures: In 1966 UNRWA set the number of refugees at 1,317,749. In fact, the number of real refugees, as calculated by Dr. Pinner, was 367,000. The difference of over 950,000 is roughly made up as follows:

Unrecorded deaths	117,000
Ex-refugees resettled in 1948	109,000
Ex-refugees who became self-supporting between 1948 and 1966 (85,000 in Syria, 60,000 in Lebanon, and 80,000 in Jordan)	225,000
Frontier villagers in Jordan (nonrefugees)	15,000

Self-appointed nonrefugees (pre–1948 residents of "West
Jordan" and the Gaza Strip registered as refugees)   484,000

Note 6. A comparison of the UNRWA figures and the 1967
Israeli census:

GAZA		WEST BANK	
UNRWA	*GOI Census	UNRWA	*GOI Census
(Dec. 31, 1967	(Provisional)	(Dec. 31, 1967	(Provisional)
319,000 (registered		285,000 (registered)	
	250,000 (registered)		180,000 (registered)
227,000 (ration recipients)		151,000 (ration recipients)	
	207,000 (a) (Household head born in Israel)		106,000 (a) (Household head born in Israel)

(a) Not included cases where the origin of the household head was
    not known.

*Government of Israel.

Note 7. In March 1971 the Ministry of Agriculture had a staff
in the West Bank of 314 local employees and 28 Israelis. Yields
of irrigated crops per area-unit improved from 50 percent to
100 percent. Farmers are permitted to borrow from the Israel
Ministry at low interest rates. As a result of thèse efforts, the
value of agricultural output in the West Bank rose from 135
million Israeli pounds in 1967–68 to 350 million Israeli pounds
in 1971–72.

The budget for vocational training in 1971–72 amounted to
700,000 Israeli pounds. Those participating in the courses received pocket money in keeping with the trades taught in sums
between 45 Israeli pounds and 75 Israeli pounds per month.

After the Israeli occupation of the West Bank and the Gaza
Strip, the percentage of men belonging to the labor force rose
from 45 percent to 66 percent and the percentage of work-
seekers gainfully employed was over 97 percent. Wages rose
from 5 Israeli pounds per day in the West Bank to 15.6 Israeli
pounds by December 1973. In Gaza, prewar daily wages had
been 3.1 Israeli pounds; they had risen to 16.7 Israeli pounds
by December 1972.

Note 8. The 1963 report further states: "It should be obvious
to anyone that the day must come when a solution—other than
international charity and status quo—must challenge the imagi-

nation and statesmanship of U.S. leaders, when this waste and this travesty must finally be discontinued." Terming the renewal of UNRWA's function a waste of millions and an abuse of human beings, I bitterly deplored the "diabolical misuse of the instrumentality of the United Nations as an abuse of its power and prestige, which were designed for peaceful, positive, and constructive purposes, as outlined in the Charter."

Note 9. The following is a chronological list of assaults by the terrorists in a program carried to all parts of the world. Besides those listed here, numerous planned attacks were aborted by police on the scene—mostly in international airports.

December 26, 1968. At *Athens Airport,* there was a gunfire attack by Arabs on an El Al plane, killing an Israeli passenger and wounding a stewardess.

February 18, 1969. At *Zurich Airport,* there was a terrorist gunfire attack on an El Al plane in which the copilot was killed and the pilot wounded.

November 27, 1969. In *Athens,* 2 Jordanians hand-grenaded the El Al office; a Greek child was killed and 13 persons were wounded.

February 10, 1970. At *Munich Airport,* 2 Jordanians and 1 Egyptian attacked an El Al plane, killing an Israeli passenger and wounding 8 others.

February 21, 1970. Over *Switzerland,* a Swissair plane exploded in midair. 47 passengers and crew members were killed, 15 of them Israelis—an Arab terrorist group claimed responsibility.

May 4, 1970. In *Paraguay,* 2 Palestinians attacked the Israeli embassy at Asuncion. The wife of an Israeli diplomat was killed, a secretary wounded.

September 6, 1970. Enroute from *Amsterdam, Frankfurt,* and *Zurich,* to New York, Arab terrorists hijacked three planes, Pan-Am, TWA and Swissair, with a total of 400 passengers. The TWA and Swissair planes were forced to land at Zerqa in Jordan, the Pan-Am plane in Cairo; all three were blown up.

May 30, 1972. At *Lod Airport,* 3 Japanese terrorists machine-gunned passengers. Of the 27 persons killed and 80 wounded, most of the victims were Puerto Rican pilgrims.

In terrorist attacks since that time, no efforts have been made by the invaded countries to penalize the terrorists who were caught. The following is a list of attacks in each country and the steps which have been taken to apprehend, hold, or punish the terrorists.

September 1972. In *Munich, West Germany,* when 11 members of the Israeli Olympic team and 5 of 8 attacking gunmen were killed, the 3 survivors were jailed to await trial. Seven weeks later, however, 2 other Palestinians hijacked a West German jetliner and won their release. All were flown to Libya. Nothing has been heard of them since.

March 1973. In *Khartoum, Sudan,* the United States ambassador to the Sudan and two other diplomats were murdered. A Sudanese court sentenced the 8 terrorists who staged the attack to life imprisonment. But the government said it was turning them over to the Palestine Liberation Organization for punishment. They turned up in Cairo under loose house arrest.

July 1973. In *Amsterdam,* 2 Palestinians, a Japanese extremist, and a Honduran leftist teamed up to hijack a Japanese jumbo jet airliner destined for Benghazi, Libya. They blew up the plane after freeing 137 hostages. Freed in August 1974, they were flown by the PLO to Damascus, where they dropped out of sight.

August 1973. In *Athens,* an Arab gunman seized several hostages in a hotel and traded them for safe-conduct to Kuwait.

Also in that month, at *Athens Airport,* 2 Palestinians carried out an attack with bombs and guns, killing 5 persons and injuring 55. A Greek court sentenced them to death, but the government reduced the sentence to life imprisonment. They were expelled on May 5, 1974 because the Government feared more terrorist attacks.

September 1973. At the Saudi Arabian embassy in *Paris,* 5 Arab gunmen held 4 persons hostage for 27 hours and took to the air in a commandeered airliner. After landing in Kuwait, they remained in jail until the October 1973 Middle East War, when they were reported shipped to a fighting front.

December 1973. In *Rome,* 5 Arab guerrillas killed 31 people at the airport and hijacked a Lufthansa airliner to Kuwait, where they gave themselves up. The Kuwaiti authorities sent them to Cairo to be turned over to the PLO. In November 1974, they were flown to Tunis at the demand of 4 Arab gunmen who seized a British airliner in Dubai and hijacked it to that country. Unpunished, it is thought that the 5 terrorists were sent on to Libya at their own request.

Bring out the books that bring in the issues.

☐ THE ISRAEL-ARAB READER, 3rd edition
   Walter Laqueur, ed.   2487 • $2.95

☐ "THEY'VE KILLED THE PRESIDENT" the search for the
   murderers of John F. Kennedy Robert Sam Anson 2525 • $2.50

☐ GUILTY, GUILTY, GUILTY G. B. Trudeau   2677 • $1.25

☐ THE PENTAGON PAPERS Neil Sheehan, Hedrick Smith,
   E. W. Kenworthy and Fox Butterfield   7255 • $2.25

☐ WHO RUNS CONGRESS? Mark J. Green,
   James M. Fallows and David R. Zwick   8151 • $2.25

☐ THE MAKING OF THE PRESIDENT, 1972
   Theodore White   8344 • $2.25

☐ THE WHITE HOUSE TRANSCRIPTS
   Gerald Gold of **The New York Times,** general ed. 8738 • $2.50

☐ QUOTATIONS FROM CHAIRMAN MAO TSE-TUNG
   Stuart A. Schram, ed.   10059 • $1.95

☐ THE ECO-SPASM REPORT Alvin Toffler   10181 • $1.75

☐ BURY MY HEART AT WOUNDED KNEE Dee Brown 10277 • $2.50

☐ SOCIALISM Michael Harrington   10907 • $2.95

Buy them at your local bookstore or use this handy coupon for ordering:

Bantam Book Catalog

Here's your up-to-the-minute listing of every book currently available from Bantam.

This easy-to-use catalog is divided into categories and contains over 1400 titles by your favorite authors.

So don't delay—take advantage of this special opportunity to increase your reading pleasure.

Just send us your name and address and 25¢ (to help defray postage and handling costs).

BANTAM BOOKS, INC.
Dept. FC, 414 East Golf Road, Des Plaines, Ill. 60016

Mr./Mrs./Miss_____
(please print)

Address_____

City_____State_____Zip_____

Do you know someone who enjoys books? Just give us their names and addresses and we'll send them a catalog too!

_____

Mr./Mrs./Miss_____

Address_____

City_____State_____Zip_____

_____

Mr./Mrs./Miss_____

Address_____

City_____State_____Zip_____

FC—6/77